Biblical Thinking for Building Healthy Churches

IX 9Marks Journal

info@9marks.org | www.9marks.org

Tools like this are provided by the generous investment of donors.
Each gift to 9Marks helps equip church leaders with a biblical vision and practical resources for displaying God's glory to the nations through healthy churches.

Donate at: www.9marks.org/donate.

Or make checks payable to "9Marks" and mail to:
9 Marks
525 A St. NE
Washington, DC 20002

Editorial Director: Jonathan Leeman
Editor: Sam Emadi
Managing Editor: Alex Duke
Layout: Rubner Durais
Cover Design: OpenBox9
Production Manager: Rick Denham
& Mary Beth Freeman
9Marks President: Mark Dever

ISBN: 9798657272079

CONTENTS

Editor's Note
The Shepherd: The Work and Character of a Pastor

Jonathan Leeman

We've been publishing the 9Marks Journal for over a decade, yet we've never done one focused on the pastor—his work and character. So let's call this Journal irresponsibly overdue. While editing it, I found myself, first, convicted; second, encouraged; and third, well supplied with tweet after tweet of wisdom. I'm confident you'll enjoy and benefit from it.

The pastor has to wear lots of hats in the course of his work: program-director, administrator, counselor, evangelist, and, at the top of the list, preacher and teacher. Yet in all of this, he is a shepherd. He watches over sheep, principally by concerning himself with their understanding of God's Word and how it applies to their life together and with outsiders.

If you're looking for background reading for this Journal, check out Paul Alexander's four-part series of biblical theology summaries on the shepherding theme throughout Scripture: part 1, part 2, part 3, and part 4. Also, see Bobby Jamieson's one-article summary on the biblical theology of shepherding here.

All that provides the whole-Bible backdrop to the pieces of this Journal, many of which focus on one biblical phrase or idea from the New Testament about a pastor's work. Matt Emadi reflects on the requirement for elders to be hospitable, Dan Miller on the command to patience, Aaron Menikoff on the call to holiness, Sam Emadi on what it means to be "able to teach," and Kevin DeYoung on not being quarrelsome.

There's nothing new, explosive, or headline-making in any of this. But it's all deep, true, essential, and re-calibrating to your life and work!

I plan on reading Ed Moore's piece on pastoring and parenting with my wife. Ray Ortlund's two pieces on what to remember when things are going well or poorly should be read with a staff or fellow elders. Ryan Fullerton's on praying for your people, Paul Martin's on generosity, Bert Daniel's on godliness, Erik Raymond's on humility, and Bob Johnson's on love should all be read monthly!

As I look over the table of contents, it's hard for me to know what to highlight because each picks up a crucial aspect of pastoral work. Let me suggest this. There are 32 articles. Try reading one a day for a month (plus 1 or 2 days), maybe after you read your Bible. Ask God to grow you and every other pastor in your city in all these ways.

Tend Your Heart: Drinking from the Fountain of Mirth

David Mathis

With palpable darkness descending over Middle-earth, and the splintered fellowship driving east toward Mordor, the hobbit Pippen observes in Gandalf a glimpse of deep, stabilizing joy—joy characteristic of good wizards and good pastors alike:

> In the wizard's face he saw at first only lines of care and sorrow; though as he looked more intently, he perceived that under all there was a great joy: a fountain of mirth enough to set a kingdom laughing, were it to gush forth.

Under all there was a great joy. Yes, indeed. Just as there had been, every step of the way, for the Man of Sorrows. Or, as the apostle Paul says, "sorrowful yet always rejoicing" (2 Cor. 6:10). And not faint joy, but a fountain. *Great joy*.

Christian pastors carry great sorrows. Not that others don't. But to be a pastor means to answer the call to bear more weights, more burdens, more cares, more sorrows. Yet the work is also not without its multiplied joys. And not just joy that is icing on the cake, but an unshakable, subterranean joy that is essential for the work of the ministry, for keeping one's balance in the most disorienting of days.

So, elders must *aspire* (1 Tim. 3:1). They must want to do the work, and then do it "with joy and not with groaning," otherwise "that would be of no advantage" to the flock (Heb. 13:17). Good pastors look beyond the barriers of their present distresses to "the glory that is going to be revealed" (1 Pet. 5:1). Laboring as a team, they remind each other, when the chief Shepherd appears, we "will receive the unfading crown of glory" (1 Pet. 5:4).

But joy is not just the promise of the future. Even now, there is a fountain of mirth. They "exercise oversight" with joy—"not for shameful gain," says Peter, "but eagerly." In fact, such ministry for joy, from joy, finds its roots in God himself: "not under compulsion, but willingly, *as God would have you*" (1 Pet. 5:2). He is our great fountain of mirth, ready to gush forth, beneath every care and sorrow in this age.

TENDING TO JOY

Joy is vital in the work of pastor-elders, and such joy does not endure or deepen apart from tending. Pastors are both well-positioned to pursue such joy and in peril of neglecting to do so. Because pastors are teachers (Eph. 4:11; 1 Tim. 2:12; 5:17; Heb. 13:7), we are in grave danger of preaching and teaching consuming our meditation. Subtly, God's Word becomes something for others rather than first and foremost for ourselves.

Undershepherds in the church are first, and most essentially, sheep. Our calling is to rejoice more that our names are written in heaven than that we're the instruments of fruitful ministry (Luke 10:20). And sheep need *to feed*. Not just to feed *others*, but to *be fed* by the chief Shepherd himself. We need to go out to pasture and fill our own spiritual stomachs, to maintain and nurture and deepen our own affection for Christ and our sense of nearness to him.

But more specifically, what is that "fountain of mirth"? What is the one well, among other sources of joy, from which the pastor must drink most deeply? It's the Book. The very words of God that we have been entrusted to teach are the very words that are vital for feeding, sustaining, and merrying our own souls. We may marshal the full range of natural and spiritual means to tend our hearts, but we cannot minimize or ignore the most fundamental elixir of spiritual vibrancy: the Word of God.

ENJOYING THE BOOK

So, as pastors, we read, study, and meditate not just for our next teaching assignment, or even with a direct eye on future ministry. We come morning by morning to our God *for food for our own soul.* We seek to gather a day's portion. We go out to pasture. We lose track of time. Later on, we'll think about what and how to teach. There's the rest of the day for that.

Healthy pastors aim to take in far more than we put out in public teaching. We want to die to any sense of thinking, *If I read it, or think it, I need to use it.* No, we don't. Pastoral ministry is not so efficient, not so American. It's human—not animal, not machine. We want our teaching ministry—in prayers, in devotions, in conservations, in counseling, in text messages, in letters, in sermons—to be just the tip of the iceberg of the movements and stirrings and delights and reverent meditations of our souls.

BE IN THE BOOK

The apostle Paul did not suffer lazy Christians (1 Thess. 5:14; 2 Thess. 3:6–15), and especially not lazy pastors (1 Tim. 4:10; 5:17–18; 1 Thess. 5:12–13). And Book work is often hard work. Paul writes to his protégé Timothy, and to all pastors, "Do your best to present yourself to God as one approved, a worker who has no need to be ashamed, rightly handling the word of truth" (2 Tim. 2:15). That right handling of God's Word begins in tending to our own hearts with the truth, long before we stand up in public to reveal them. Christ means for his undershepherds to be men of his Book—not mere academics of it but enjoyers of it.

Paul tells Timothy, and us, to devote ourselves "to the public reading of Scripture, to exhortation, to teaching" (1 Tim. 4:13). "Practice these things," he says, "*immerse yourself in them*, so that all may see your progress" (1 Tim. 4:15). Do our people see our progress over time, not because we're studying to impress, but because we're tending to our hearts in unhurried, even leisurely meditation in this Book? Is our love for God himself, through his words, becoming increasingly contagious?

"Immerse yourself in them"—literally, "be in them." Brothers, let's *be in the Bible.* We can't commend what we don't cherish. We can't teach well, and for long, what we're not immersing ourselves in. To be a pastor is to be called to "be in" the word of God, without leave. To be ready in season and out (2 Tim. 4:2).

KEEP A CLOSE WATCH

Tending to our hearts doesn't mean peeling at the layers of our internal, subjective hearts with amateur analyses. It means standing daily before the reflecting glass of God's Word for the sake of our own souls (Jas. 1:23–25).

And in tending to ourselves with the words of God, we guard our teaching and our people from error—both the error of untrue words and the error of an undue demeanor in handling God's Word. As we tend to our own hearts with the truths of heaven, we are not ignoring our people but caring well for them. The two go hand in hand. Paul said to the Ephesian elders: "Pay careful attention to yourselves and to all the flock" (Acts 20:28). And he said to Timothy who was in Ephesus:

> Keep a close watch on yourself and on the teaching. Persist in this, for by so doing you will save both yourself and your hearers. (1 Tim. 4:16)

Brothers, we have permission to set aside our next sermon, open the Book, and simply tend to our own heart for an unhurried season each day. Indeed we have a call—to drink at the fountain of mirth. Our people need leaders with great joy under all the many cares and sorrows.

ABOUT THE AUTHOR
David Mathis is executive editor for desiringGod.org and pastor at Cities Church in Minneapolis/St. Paul.

Why Should Pastors Care About Their Holiness?

Aaron
Menikoff

"Vigilance" has to be the war-cry of every pastor. "The true Christian is called to be a soldier," wrote J. C. Ryle, "and must behave as such from the day of his conversion to the day of his death."[1] Pastors face a myriad of temptations. All are common—idleness, lust, and anger. Some are made sharper by the unique nature of a pastor's work—pride, discontentment, and impatience stand out.

This article is a charge for every pastor to soldier on. Why should a pastor care about his personal holiness? Here are three straightforward answers.

1. BECAUSE EVERY PASTOR IS A CHRISTIAN

The battle against sin is lost when the pastor thinks he is in a separate class, impervious from the spiritual warfare faced by all believers. First and foremost, he must see himself as a Christian who must endure to the end.

Scripture is clear. Each believer is a new creation and must live a new and holy life (2 Cor. 5:17). Like a tree, the true believer will bear spiritual fruit (Rom. 7:4). The real Christian is dead to his sin and cannot live in it (Rom. 6:2). After all, the unrighteous won't inherit God's kingdom (1 Cor. 6:9). The Christian's righteousness is the eternal plan of God who ordained holiness for each of his elect (Eph. 1:4).

Pastor, you know better than anyone the temptation to merely *appear* godly (2 Tim. 3:3). You stand up every week before a congregation who expects you to exemplify Christian virtue. Don't excuse yourself from the fight, not for a second. Holiness is not a mask we wear; it's the path we walk. This is true for the pastor because it is true for every Christian.

2. BECAUSE EVERY PASTOR IS AN EXAMPLE

Though every pastor is first and foremost a Christian, there is no doubt the pastor is a *leading* Christian. He is to lead out in holiness, modeling for the church what a disciple of Jesus Christ looks like. The pastor must be *more* vigilant against sin, *more* aware of his temptation, and *more* committed to personal holiness.

The church fundamentally depends on Christ and his atoning work. This is the primary truth. Nonetheless, to a lesser but still very real degree, the church leans into the faithfulness of the pastor.

We find, for example, special requirements in Scripture for pastors to be godly. Paul commanded the Ephesian elders and, by extension, all elders to "pay careful attention" to their lives (Acts 20:28). Paul called the minister's life holy, righteous, and blameless (1 Thess. 2:10). He urged Timothy to have a "good conscience" (1 Tim. 1:5, 19) and warned this young pastor against participating in the sins of others (1 Tim. 5:22). Paul summed up his counsel by asserting the pastor must flee sin and "pursue righteousness" (1 Tim. 6:11).

---

1 J. C. Ryle, *Holiness: Its Nature, Hindrances, Difficulties, and Roots* (Chicago: Moody, 2010), 111.

Christians don't learn how to be holy simply by reading the Bible. They are to look at the example set by their pastors. Paul told the Corinthians, Philippians, and Thessalonians to imitate him (1 Cor. 4:16–17; 11:1; Phil. 4:9; 1 Thess. 1:6; 2 Thess. 3:7–9). He told Timothy to set an example for the Ephesians "in speech, in conduct, in love, in faith, in purity" (1 Tim. 4:12). He instructed Titus to be "a model of good works" (Titus 2:7). He made special lists of elder qualifications that start with the call to be "above reproach" (1 Tim. 3:1–7; Titus 1:6–9). In fact, the New Testament expectation is that the elders will be so known for their holiness that it would be ridiculous to accept an allegation against them unless there are multiple accusers (1 Tim. 5:19).

Simply put, the call to pastoral ministry is a call to holiness. If you doubt this for a moment, consider 1 Timothy 4:16: "Keep a close watch on yourself and on the teaching. Persist in this, for by so doing you will save both yourself and your hearers." We are right to attribute salvation to Christ alone, but if we neglect to factor in the role of the pastor we have diminished the office we are privileged to hold. John Calvin addressed this unusual reality:

> A pastor will become even more zealous when he is told that both his salvation and that of the people who listen to him depend on his devotion to his office... God alone saves, and no part of his glory can be transferred to men. But God's glory is not at all diminished when he employs men's efforts to bestow salvation... God alone is the author of salvation. But this does not exclude the ministry of men, for the well-being of the church depends on that ministry.[2]

Brothers, heed Paul's charge: "Keep a close watch on yourself." Don't let a day go by without pleading with God to fill you to overflowing with the fruit of his Holy Spirit. This holiness is required not only for your sake, but for the sake of the church God has given you to lead.

3. BECAUSE EVERY PASTOR IS AN INTERCESSOR.

After calling on the sick to ask the elders to pray over them, James said holiness is the fuel of an effective prayer: "The prayer of a righteous person has great power as it is working" (James 5:16). This is why Peter charged his readers to "be self-controlled and sober-minded for the sake of your prayers" (1 Pet. 4:7).

For the sake of your prayers.

Read through the New Testament and you'll quickly discover God uses the prayers of Christian leaders to grow his churches. Paul prayed the congregation in Philippi would have a love that abounds "more and more, with knowledge and with all discernment" (Phil. 1:9). He prayed the Ephesians would be "strengthened with power" and "grounded in love" and "filled with all the fullness of God" (Eph. 3:14–19). He prayed the Colossians would be "filled with the knowledge of [God's] will (Col. 1:9) and that the Thessalonians would "walk in a manner worthy of God" (1 Thess. 2:12).

As I write these words in 2020, some churches are only beginning to gather after the COVID-19 quarantine. Loneliness is rampant. Most churches are struggling to know how to respond to the killings of African-Americans and the ensuing riots. I'm witnessing on social media accusations of wokism and racism. The church is hurting.

Nearly twenty years ago, D. A. Carson listed several urgent needs faced by the church. At the top of the list he put our inattention to God: "We are not captured by his holiness and love; his thoughts and words capture too little of our imagination, too little of our discourse, too few of our priorities." Knowing God, Carson insisted, was our biggest challenge. He argued the chief way to address this problem is "spiritual, persistent, biblically minded prayer."[3]

I couldn't agree more, but I would make one additional recommendation. We need holy pastors leading the way in prayer.

I don't have all the answers to today's serious problems, but I'm

---

2 John Calvin, *1 & 2 Timothy* in *The Crossway Classic Commentaries,* ed. Alister McGrath and J. I. Packer (Wheaton, Ill.: Crossway, 1998), 78.

3 D. A. Carson, *A Call to Spiritual Reformation: Priorities from Paul and His Prayers* (Grand Rapids, Mich.: Baker Books, 1992), 15–16.

convinced part of the solution is pastors on their knees. Yes, the church needs men of God preaching the gospel. We need pastor-theologians grappling with arguments belittling penal substitutionary atonement. We need to work through implications of the gospel as they relate to issues of racism. But God will only bless this work if there are pastors so changed by the gospel they are "self-controlled and sober-minded" for the sake of their prayers and the salvation of their churches.

Brother pastor, do you care about holiness? My guess is you do, otherwise you wouldn't have reached the end of this article! Please don't give up caring. Be vigilant. Soldier on against your sin from this day to the day of your death.

ABOUT THE AUTHOR
Aaron Menikoff is the senior pastor of Mt. Vernon Baptist Church in Sandy Springs, Georgia.

What Does It Mean to Be "Qualified" for Ministry?

Bobby Scott

In 1 Timothy 3:1–6 and in Titus 1:5–9, God requires that pastors conform to an uncompromising, holy standard. When it comes to being qualified for this sacred and high calling, it's easy to say with Paul, "Who is adequate for these things?" (2 Cor. 2:16). The resounding answer is "No one!"— That is, no one apart from God's enabling grace. Paul clarifies, "Not that we are sufficient in ourselves to claim anything as coming from us, but our sufficiency is from God, who has made us sufficient to be ministers of a new covenant" (2 Cor. 3:5–6). Therefore, by God's grace all shepherds can and must meet these qualifications.

The rest of this article will define God's qualifications for pastoral ministry, explain the process of raising up men to meet these standards, and then consider why pastors must live by these standards for the spiritual health of the church.

WHAT ARE THE BIBLICAL QUALIFICATIONS FOR A PASTOR?

Except for the ability to teach, every pastoral qualification focuses on character. These qualifications are not snapshots of a man's life but characteristics—consistent patterns of his life.

The qualifications in 1 Timothy 3:1–6 and Titus 1:5–9 tell the story of a godly leader. What is he like in his home? Is he a one-woman man? Does he have the skill to lead relationally? If not, then he cannot lead the church. What is his reputation with unbelievers on his job and in his community? He must be godly Monday through Saturday, not just religious on Sunday. Is he a bully, or is he loving and kind?

Of course, no one aspiring to be a pastor should declare himself qualified. The church must assess and affirm his character. Without the evidence of these grace-produced qualities in his life, the church must not affirm that a man is fit for this sacred office. Charisma and talent cannot be used as criteria to supplant character and faithfulness.

HOW CAN MEN BECOME QUALIFIED?

God calls leaders (1 Tim. 3:1) and gifts the church with them (Eph. 4:11). But before they serve, they must be equipped. Jesus called the twelve and sent them out to preach, but not until he first spent time with them to train them (Mark 3:13–14).

Seminaries may provide wonderful training opportunities, but pastors ultimately learn to pastor from other pastors. Paul saw God's grace in young Timothy, so he mentored him (Acts 16:3), demonstrating the grace-produced character of a qualified life (2 Tim. 3:11–12). Men must be shown what it means to be godly leaders. Therefore, pastors must use Paul's list in 1 Timothy 3:1–6 as a discipling guide to prepare men for ministry. Conversely, pastors must use Paul's list in Titus to keep unqualified men away from the pastorate. The bottom line is that every man who serves the church as a pastor must live a life characterized by Paul's list of qualifications.

WHY MUST CHURCHES REQUIRE THAT THEIR PASTORS MEET PAUL'S LIST OF QUALIFICATIONS?

Well, the simple answer is because God says so. God speaks through his Word, and his Word says that pastors *must be* men who meet these standards.

Furthermore, the church is God's. He purchased it with his own blood (Acts 20:28), so God sets the standard for who leads it. The command *must be* is the leading verb throughout the list of qualifications. God didn't leave the pastor's job description for churches to determine. He wrote them himself, and they are non-negotiable. The man of God *must be* blameless. His life *must be* free from legitimate scandal and positively conform to the qualifications set by God. Where leaders lead, people follow. Leaders therefore *must be* blameless because God desires blamelessness of all of his people (Phil. 2:15).

Through his death and resurrection Jesus reconciles rebels to live in a holy, loving union with the Father. Christ raises up leaders and gives them as gifts to the church to show believers how to do that (Phil. 3:17)—how to live holy lives that please their holy God.

My dearly beloved pastors, it matters how we live. May the measureless love of our Father, who gave us his holy Son to save us from our sin, fill our hearts so that we delight in pursuing holiness. In the end, people will be like their leaders, and Jesus died to make his people, his bride, holy. Therefore, let every church say "amen," and let every true church pray for and raise up godly pastors whose lives adorn the gospel of grace. In our tumultuous times of dark distress, may our churches radiate with the brilliance of the glory of his grace, that we might all appear as lights of Christ's saving and sanctifying power.

ABOUT THE AUTHOR

Bobby Scott is a co-pastor of Community of Faith Bible Church in South Gate, California.

Gifted and Godly... But Especially Godly

Bert Daniel

Should a church require that a pastor be gifted? Yes. Paul indicates that if a man desires to serve as a pastor, he must be "able to teach" (1 Tim. 3:2; Tit. 1.9). A man is not required to produce theological tomes for the ages or to pack out auditoriums with his great oratorical skills, but he must be able to faithfully and clearly communicate the truth of Scripture so that others are able to understand the Bible and act upon it.

What's equally noteworthy, however, is the unmistakable emphasis that Paul places on the necessity of a pastor's godliness. He spends more ink here than he does on giftedness. For Paul, godliness is of utmost importance.

For example, in 1 Timothy 3:1–7, Paul lists approximately sixteen qualifications for a man who desires to serve as an overseer. One relates to giftedness: the ability to teach. Fifteen refer to character.

Likewise, in Titus 1:5–9, Paul lists approximately sixteen qualifications for a pastor. One relates to giftedness: again, the ability to instruct in sound doctrine. Fifteen address character.

Paul is undeniably biased. Giftedness matters. Character matters maybe more.

Consequently, Paul insists that the young pastor, Timothy, prioritize godliness in his life and ministry. Paul charges Timothy: "Train yourself for godliness" (1 Tim. 4:7); "keep yourself pure" (1 Tim. 5:22); "flee youthful passions and pursue righteousness, faith, love, and peace along with those who call on the Lord from a pure heart" (2 Tim. 2:22).

WHY GODLINESS?

Why does Paul emphasize godliness over giftedness?

It's not that the gospel life is more important than the gospel word. How many passages throughout the pastoral epistles emphasize faithful teaching! Again, the gospel word must come first. Yet beyond that basic element of faithfully teaching the gospel word, maybe Paul realizes that human beings generally don't need any help in being persuaded to follow charismatic and talented leaders. We do it naturally.

What we—even as Christians—fail to recognize is how essential godliness in the life of the pastor is to gospel-word ministry.

In Titus 2:11–14, Paul writes, "For the grace of God has appeared, bringing salvation for all people, training us to renounce ungodliness... and to live... godly lives... waiting for our blessed hope, the appearing of the glory of our great God and Savior Jesus Christ, who gave himself for us to redeem us from all lawlessness and to purify for himself a people for his own possession who are zealous for good works." According to Paul, God graciously redeems his people so that they might reject ungodliness and reflect his character to the world.

Therefore, godliness is mission-critical for the church. And, like any group of people, churches will take on the character of their leaders. More times than not, ungodly pastors will produce ungodly churches, and godly pastors will give rise to godly churches. As a result, pastors, whom God calls to lead this band of transformed repenters, must be characterized by repentance and an ongoing pursuit of godliness.

For this reason, the church so desperately needs leaders who not only teach the truth clearly and compellingly but also who live it authentically and consistently. Paul warns that there will be those who "have the appearance of godliness, but deny its power" (2 Tim. 3:5). Perhaps these individuals grew up in the church; perhaps they know some Bible verses; perhaps they advocate family values—but they've never been transformed by the gospel. So many spiritual counterfeits exist that the church needs to be led by men who are living examples of the transforming power of the gospel.

PASTORS AS EXAMPLES

Pastors also serve as examples to their flock. Paul speaks plainly on this point: "Set the believers an example in speech, in conduct, in love, in faith, in purity" (1 Tim. 4:12). And again Paul directs, "Show yourself in all respects to be a model of good works, and in your teaching show integrity, dignity, and sound speech" (Tit. 2:7–8).

Therefore, pastors, prioritize the pursuit of godliness in your life.

Consistent time alone with God in his Word and in prayer are of the utmost importance.

Be accountable to other men.

Accept that most pastors possess average gifts, and resolve to be happy to be a man who possesses average gifts and a biblical zeal for godliness.

Be encouraged. God will not finally evaluate our ministries based on the measure of our giftedness. God will finally evaluate our ministries based on our diligence to exercise the gifts he has given us and on our faithfulness to know him and to walk with him before our people.

CONCLUSION

Brothers, let's strive to be men like Paul who on the one hand says, "I am the chief of sinners" (1 Tim. 1:15), and other the other hand says, "You . . . have followed my teaching, my conduct, my aim in life, my faith, my patience, my love, my steadfastness" (2 Tim. 3:10).

In other words, let us say with Paul, "I am an example of a sinner transformed by the power of the gospel, and I am a man whose life, though imperfectly, does in fact genuinely and increasingly reflect the character of God to God's people." For Robert Murray McCheyne's words still ring true: "My people's greatest need is my own personal holiness."

ABOUT THE AUTHOR
Bert Daniel is the pastor of Crawford Avenue Baptist Church in Augusta, Georgia.

Right and Wrong Pastoral Ambitions

Phil Newton

Ambitions are tricky. Functioning well, they motivate to action, pursue the worthwhile, steer away from the ignoble, and provide energy to persevere. Yet pride, selfishness, bitterness, and a host of sins, like parasites, sicken once healthy ambitions toward destructiveness. In guarding our hearts, we must also guard our ambitions.

Pastoral calling and ministry training do not inoculate from wrong ambitions. But men who are humbly lashed to God's Word, with character shaped by the gospel, will pursue right ambitions.

Jesus alone had entirely pure ambitions, evident in his obedience, focus, and selfless love. He obediently sought to do the Father's will (John 8:28; John 4:34; Ps. 40:8; Heb. 10:7); focused on his Father's mission, even when the crowds wanted to make him king; and demonstrated selfless love toward his followers, laying down his life as a substitute for sinners (John 15:13).

As pastors, we can learn from this. If we want to reorder out pastoral ambitions, then we must emulate Christ.

What does this look like when it plays out into real-life, pastoral settings? Let's think about it by considering two wrong and two right ambitions.

WRONG AMBITIONS FOR PASTORS

1. This church needs me to get them in shape.

It goes like this. "I'm tired of seeing so many bad churches and carnal people. I know what a church needs to look like. I'll shape people up or ship them out." During college, I watched a pastor squeeze people into his "brand" of Christianity, complete with a list of dos and don'ts to be in his favor. Staff and church members feared him and his heavy-handedness. He got what he wanted but it lacked grace.

Some churches might cross their "T's" and dots their "I's" with the best of them. But they've sim-ply been hammered into shape by an authoritarian pastor. Such pastors haven't listened to Peter; they domineer and lord over the flock (1 Pet. 5:3). They've ignored Paul; they bully and push their weight around to keep the church conformed to their ideas (Titus 1:7). They've neglected John's warning; like Diotrephes, they "love to be first," refuse counsel, and spend inordinate time criticizing ministers who don't applaud them (3 John 9–10, NASB). They might be successful when it comes to nickels and noses, but they fail miserably in reproducing healthy disciples. Richard Sibbes counseled, "The ambassadors of so gentle a Saviour should not be overbearing, setting up themselves in the hearts of people where Christ alone should sit as in his own temple."

2. With my gifts, I can build this church.

I knew a pastor whose membership grew enormously under his leadership. He was a gifted organizer, worked tirelessly, mastered programs, and regimented his staff. The denomination applauded him. He had plenty of people but he didn't faithfully preach Christ. He built the church on his organizational gifts. He "succeeded" in numbers but neglected to establish his church on the gospel. He had accidentally, I assume, erected a monument to his own skills. Years later, it imploded. His "gifts" were too weak to hold the church together. This is no surprise. If our gifts hold the church together, then it's built on shifting sand (Matt. 7:24–27).

Others may preach God's Word but fail to personally apply what they're preaching. In doing so, they build the church on pulpit ability. Crafting masterful sermons, such men love attention, feed on notoriety, and shape ministry to center on their gifts. Numerous times, I've heard church members *oohh* and *aahh* over a pastor's preaching skills, only later to shrivel on the vine due to him making church about his performance. Preaching gifts can easily hide wrong ambitions. That's why Paul's preaching aimed to demonstrate the Spirit and power, "so that your faith would not rest in the wisdom of men, but in the power of God" (1 Cor. 2:4–5).

RIGHT AMBITIONS
FOR PASTORS

1. By God's grace, I seek to live as a follower of Jesus Christ.

As Timothy labored in pastoral responsibilities at Ephesus, with insistence to teach and exhort the church, Paul told him, "Let no one despise you for your youth, but set the believers an example in speech, in conduct, in love, in faith, in purity" (1 Tim. 4:11–12). Before focus on preaching, give attention to living as Jesus' follower. Model discipleship. Paul set a standard for pastors to emulate. "Be imitators of me, as I am of Christ" (1 Cor. 11:1; Heb. 13:7). Similarly, Peter charged the elders to shepherd God's flock, "being examples to the flock" (1 Pet. 5:3).

Every now and then, someone will ask me what to look for in a senior pastor. I always tell them not to overlook the obvious. The New Testament gives more attention to a pastor's character than his duties. We do want gifted men who will labor in expositional preaching. But first, we want holy men. Derek Tidball, commenting on Paul's aim with Timothy and Titus, notes, "He was concerned about their achieving the task, but was even more concerned about the kind of people they were." Major on faithful preaching and shepherding, but foremost, major on living as an example of Christlikeness to the church.

2. By God's grace, I will lead the church to make much of Christ and his gospel.

Churches have personalities. Often, they reflect the passions and proclivities of their pastoral leadership. A pastor concerned with his legacy or status among peers tends to build a church around himself. Those focused on size tend to resort to faddish practices, with the church joining in as part of a carnival. The church, then, is about the pastor—his sayings, his mannerisms, his jokes and stories and clever remarks and catchy sermon outlines. Sadly, the congregation never tires of admiration. His ego grows. He believes the press reports. But where is the beauty of Christ as all in all? Nowhere to be found.

The New Testament paints a different picture. Healthy churches are centered on Christ and the gospel, never on the pastor and his programs or prominence. When Jesus first mentions the church, he emphasizes that it is *his*, which *he* builds and *he* defends and to whom *he* delegates authority (Matt. 16:13–20). The church's foundation is Christ himself (1 Cor. 3:10–11), who is also the cornerstone by which every detail is shaped and governed (Eph. 2:19–22). He purchased it with his own blood, a truth which the gospel declares (Act 20:28; Rom. 3:19–26; Eph. 1:7–12). He calls the church his bride who will dwell with him forever (Eph. 5:22–33; Rev. 21:9–14). For eternity, the church will fall before her Savior with worship and praise (Rev. 5:9–10).

Because of this, the pastor's primary ambition must be to make much of Jesus and his gospel. When the Reformers described what constituted a true church, they focused on the gospel and the ordinances. John Calvin wrote in his *Institutes*, "Wherever we see the Word of God purely preached and heard, and the sacraments administered according to Christ's institution, there, it is not to be doubted, a church of God exists." The Word "purely preached" referred to what Calvin called "the heavenly doctrine" that "has been enjoined upon the pastors" to preach. He cannot make the church about himself or he will be derelict. As Paul reminds the Corinthians, "For what we proclaim is not ourselves, but Jesus Christ as Lord with ourselves as your servants for Jesus' sake" (2 Cor. 4:5). We must forget neither our message nor our status. Jesus is Lord; pastors are servants.

More ambitions, right and wrong, surface day-by-day in the pastor's mind. Here are a few questions to help assess them:

- Do my ambitions call attention to myself or Jesus?
- Does this pursuit magnify or cloud the gospel of Christ?
- Does this ambition exalt Jesus while humbling me?
- Will this ambition shepherd or manipulate the flock?
- Does this ambition require the Spirit's power to accomplish?

Let us guard pastoral ambition by keeping in mind our standing before the Lord in judgment. May we share the same ambition as Paul, "whether at home or absent, to be pleasing to him" (2 Cor. 5:9, NASB).

ABOUT THE AUTHOR

Phil Newton is the senior pastor of South Woods Baptist Church in Memphis, Tennessee.

Parenting Advice for Pastors

Ed Moore

Mark Twain once said, "When I was a boy of 14, my father was so ignorant I could hardly stand to have the old man around. But when I got to be 21, I was astonished at how much the old man had learned in 7 years."

That's not just a humorous quote; it's a profound truth. The truth is this: wise parents do not perform in order to gain the applause of their immature, foolish children. They do what they know to be true and right—and in time, they believe their children will come along to the same conclusion. King Solomon put it this way in Proverbs 22:6: "Train up a child in the way he should go and even when he is old he will not depart from it."

What Mark Twain and Solomon assume is that parents know what is good and right. They know the way to go. We cannot make this assumption, however, in the third decade of the 21st century.

So, with that in mind, I would like to give you eight actions to consider as you raise your children in the way that they should go. These eight things aren't an exhaustive list; it's a limited list, a personal list, a subjective list. These are eight of the building blocks we used to raise our family. Indeed, most of what I would tell you is born out of failure and not out of success. Truth comes through the Word of God (John 17:17), but I am going to tell you our experiences in order to let you know that this isn't a theoretical thing drawn up in a laboratory. I haven't mastered these things. I'm telling you them because I've gone to the school of hard knocks, and I have earned a PhD.

I also don't want to put this list forward as a formula—that if you do this, your children will turn out a certain way. I've seen parents who have done everything wrong, and yet their children turned out to be polite, godly, and great people. I've seen parents who did everything by the book, and yet their kids turned out rebellious, ungodly, and unproductive. All of this is 100 percent dependent on the grace of God. Of course, this doesn't mean you contribute nothing to the success or failure of your children. But I'm stressing we are ultimately dependent on the sovereign grace of God. This should humble the proud parent and encourage the discouraged parent.

What I am about to give you is the experience of the Moore family. My family is not your family. Your family is unique; don't try to be another family. Listen to these points with a discerning ear and apply them by grace as they relate to you. I'm hoping there will be a few things that you can apply for your family. Some of the main mistakes I've made in parenting have come from trying to make apples to apples comparisons between my family and other families I saw that were doing things well. Don't do that.

So I give you these eight points, in no particular order, except that Point #8 is the most important.

Talk with your children and let them know you absolutely love and adore them. As 1 Thessalonians 5:11 says, "Encourage one another and build one another up." Apply this principle to the home. Encourage your children greatly simply by telling the all the time that you love them.

I can't tell you the number of people who have sat in my office for counseling who have said, "My father never told me that he loved me." Or they'll say something like this: "My father never told me he loved me, but I knew he did because he showed he loved me. But I wish he had told me more often." Or even if the father will say the words "I love you," the child is still left with a life-long quest to earn the father's approval. They feel like they've failed to get their dad to be pleased with them. All this can be taken care if you use expressive words with obnoxious frequency to communicate love.

Let's take the greatest example of a Father ever: God the Father. As he is looking down out of heaven at his Son, his only Son, on multiple occasions—his baptism, his transfiguration—he publicly and unashamedly says, "This is my beloved son in whom I am well pleased." "I love him and I am pleased with him."

That's how our Heavenly Father expresses his love for his Son. If we are to be godly, then we need to express our love to our children. Our Father leaves us no doubt as to whether or not he loves us. He shows us that he loves us, and demonstrated his love in that while we were yet sinners Christ died for us.

But he also *told us with words* that he loves us. There are 1189 chapters of the Bible—and he just keeps saying it over and over again.

How does this apply practically? Tell your children frequently that you love them. This might be challenging if feel you are "old school" and not that expressive. Well, "old school" is bad school in this instance. Being quiet and reserved has nothing to do with expressing love.

Over time, if you don't express love to your children, it can have a destructive effect. People wonder all the time about what they can do to make their fathers pleased with them. I can tell you what you can do to correct that problem: use expressive words with obnoxious frequency to communicate love.

My father never had a father. His father left when he was 6-months-old. My dad was the only kid in town without a father. He had no model in front of him at all. I've heard guys blame their bad dad for their being a bad dad. But I say that's hogwash. My dad had no idea how to be a dad. All he knew was that he loved his kids, and he said it all the time.

He said, "I love you. I'm thankful to be your dad. I'm proud of you." Every night before I went to sleep, he would put his hand on my head, he would kiss me, and he would tell me he loved me. He said everything that needed to be said every single day.

So, every day, tell your kids you love them. It's a godly thing to do.

I almost left this point out because it's not that spiritual. The point is "have fun!" Ecclesiastes 10:4 says, "There is a time to laugh and a time to dance." The family is the place where this should be seen the most. If heaven is a place of joy, should we not model that in the home? The home should be full of joy. If your only emphasis in parenting is what your kids cannot do, if your house is a place that never has fun, is it any wonder they leave the house when older to have fun?

In our family, we've created traditions. For example, on July 4, we go into Manhattan all wearing the same Old Navy t-shirts. And then we take goofy photos with strangers. We've had Bible reading traditions. Every year, on the night before baseball's Opening Day, no matter where we are, we sit down and watch *Field of Dreams* like we did when they were kids. I send my kids postcards. We play mini-golf tournaments. When traditions like this become part of a family, this is what it communicates: "this family is a big deal to me and it is a joy to have fun with you."

We do these things to create an atmosphere of fun and delight. It doesn't take a lot of money. You can get more mileage out of one wrestling match on the bed than a thousand trips to Disney World. My father always told me the best events in life aren't planned, are inexpensive if not free, and are some of the greatest delights in life.

I remember many years ago, one night during the Christmas season, we decided to go Christmas caroling, just us. To this day, my kids remember that. It wasn't planned; it didn't cost any money. But they will remember things like that forever. When you're having a good time, you really don't' realize how good of a time you are having. When it passes, it is gone. It's the dad's job to commemorate and draw attention to it as a big deal—with gratefulness to God. I want to demonstrate to my kids that this is a big deal because we are together. So use creative actions with enthusiastic spontaneity to create memories.

3. USE FERVENT PRAYER WITH TENACIOUS PERSISTENCE TO CONVEY HUMILITY.

It's a very simple point: humble people pray and proud people don't. If you want humble children, then you want to be humble because God gives grace to the humble. Therefore, you must pray. Pray with them, pray for them, and teach them to pray. When someone is sick, we must pause where we are and pray. Frequently, on hospital visits, I'd take one of my children with me to the bedside to pray with someone who was ill. Before you discipline your children, pray with them. Pray before bedtime. Pray 1 Thessalonians 5:1 "without ceasing" because the effectual, fervent prayer of a righteous man availeth much. If a child grows up in a home where prayer is just spoken of and never done, then why do you think the child will become one who prays themselves?

Prayer is not only the means by which we get our requests granted; it's also how we commune with God. In 1976, my brother was diagnosed with cancer. I can remember the way my parents dealt with that (thank God, my brother is alive and well today). Cancer research back in those days wasn't what is today, so our family was frightened. But I remember the way they prayed, how they called upon God. My dad was a radio announcer, and so he would often be asked to go and speak at churches, usually small churches in rural Pennsylvania. Every time he would go and speak, he would go into the men's room, he would get down on his knees, and he would bow his face to the floor, crying out to God saying, "Oh, God, please help me tonight as I speak." I wouldn't be the same as my father today, theologically speaking, but I saw the man dependent upon God in prayer.

You don't just want your kids to see you as someone who pretends to pray or only ever talks about praying. You can't fake it for that long. Instead, you need to use prayer in order to convey humility.

4. USE PRECIOUS TIME WITH STRATEGIC URGENCY IN ORDER TO MINIMIZE REGRET.

Life, like football, is a timed game. Moses tells us in Psalm 90:12: "Teach us to number our days so that we might gain heart of wisdom." If life is a timed game, then it's a quick timed game. You might get 70 years. If James calls *that* a vapor, then how short is the time you have with your kids? How short is the time when you actually have any influence over them? Your kids will come back to visit, but they don't come back to move in.

We homeschooled our children, not because we were afraid of NYC public schools or for educational purposes, but for one reason: we really liked spending time with them. When we realized how much of our day was apart from them, we simply wanted them around more.

"Children are a heritage from the Lord" (Psalm 127:3). If you don't capitalize on the few seconds you have with them, you will wake up on day like Tevia in *Fiddler on the Roof*:

> Is this the little girl I carried? Is this the little boy at play? I don't remember growing older. When did they?... Sunrise, sunset. Swiftly flow the days.

There's coming a day when your young kids don't want dad to sleep in their bed—or don't ask you to play G.I. Joes. We have tiny windows of opportunity. You will regret wasting this time. So make the best use of the time when their hearts are pliable, when they love their dads. Don't say you'll get to it another time—they grow up and they are gone. Capitalize on the time you have with your children.

5. USE SINCERE THANKSGIVING WITH PEACEFUL CONTENTMENT IN ORDER TO TEACH PROVIDENCE.

I think the most valuable thing we own is a working knowledge of the providence of God. I wonder how people who don't believe in the sovereignty of God—over both the good and the bad—don't lose their mind. Why should anything work out if it's all random?

But we believe that God is in charge, that the Lord gives and takes away. Teach your kids the practical value of resting in his providence by being thankful. Have a thankful heart and be content, especially when the ball doesn't bounce your way. Temper and anger and impatience and complaining and fault-finding are the opposite of this. "The wrath of man does not produce the righteousness of God" (James 1:20). Listen to your children talk to one another and see if they talk like you. I've had to correct how my boys spoke to one another while admitting and repenting of the ways I've spoken critically and in anger.

What helped me in this area was understanding this simple yet profound truth: the gospel is for believers. The gospel isn't only the means by which we are saved, it's the means by which we grow. "As you have received Christ Jesus the Lord, so walk in him" (Colossians 2:6).

Every aspect of the Christian life is attached to the gospel. I was an angry and impatient man. But a dramatic change came in my heart when I realized that the gospel is for believers. Things aren't going to go well all the time. When they don't, you have an amazing opportunity in front of you. It's a test from God in order for you demonstrate before your family that you trust him and his providence—and that you will do it all with sincere thanksgiving.

6. USE JOYFUL HOSPITALITY WITHOUT PETTY GRUMBLING IN ORDER TO DEMONSTRATE SELFLESSNESS.

"Show hospitality without grumbling" (1 Peter 4:9). Our home is often open to the whole church. There have been more nights when people slept at our house who were not a part of our family than nights when we were alone. We like to have people over. We like to receive guests. Exposing our children to missionaries and pastors from all over the world has been wonderful.

But what about when the guests don't know when to leave? What happens when someone breaks something? Then we have to ask ourselves, "Do we really want to show hospitality without grumbling?" Then you have the opportunity to show your children the love of Christ. These people are here as our guests, and so we show them hospitality to the glory of God. We accelerate our kids' growth in selflessness by allowing them to participate in the hospitality.

Recently, we helped someone flying through NYC who needed a place to stay. But when they showed up at our door, we found out they also had a dog. In more than 25 years, there's never been a dog inside our house! So, what were we going to do? By God's grace, we showed hospitality without grumbling, even when it was outside our comfort zone.

This is easy to preach in theory but hard to do practically. But when we think of how our Heavenly Father has welcomed us, we have the chance to show our children this kind of selfless love. Maybe they have to give up their bed and sleep on the floor. Maybe they have to work harder to prepare a meal or do the dishes. Hospitality is a great way to teach your children selflessness.

7. DISCIPLINE WITH FAITHFUL CONSISTENCY IN ORDER TO ERADICATE FOOLISHNESS.

A few verses from Proverbs:

- "Folly is bound up in the heart of a child, but the rod of discipline drives it far from him." (22:15)
- "Do not withhold discipline from a child, for if you strike him with the rod he will not die. If you strike him from the rod, you will save his soul from the grave." (23:13–14)
- "Whoever spares the rod hates his son but he who loves him is diligent to discipline him." (13:24)
- "The rod and reproof give wisdom but a child left to himself brings shame to his mother." (29:15)

Let me say a couple of things here. My wife and I did a very poor job of disciplining our children until we read Ted Tripp's book *Shepherding a Child's Heart*. Up until that point, we had used every worldly manipulative mechanism in order to discipline our children. "I'm going to count to three" or "you're making daddy so sad" or "I promise you I'm going to discipline you now."

You can make these empty threats—"if you keep doing that I'm going to take you home"—but when you do this, you aren't really teaching your kids to obey.

This is how it worked for us. I'd ask them, "Do you know what you did wrong?" They say, "yes, I didn't take out the trash." I'd say, "Do you know what I'm going to do now?" They'd say, "yes, you're going to discipline me." Afterward, I would have them sit on my lap, and I would pray with them.

Why do you do this? To be in charge? No. To get your own frustration and anger out of your system? No, never. You do this to eradicate foolishness.

8. USE THE PRACTICAL GOSPEL WITH PERSONAL APPLICATIONS IN ORDER TO REPRODUCE DISCIPLES.

If you added up the importance of everything I've said so far, it would not be as important as this last point. Show them how the grace of God works. You show kids how to do stuff—math, basketball, how to drive, etc. So teach them how the grace of God works. They need the grace of God when you are dead and gone. So teach them the gospel—that Christ died accordance with the Scriptures, that he was buried and raised. And teach them the implications of the gospel. Teach them what it means to be saved. Evangelize them. Then teach them how the gospel is for sanctification and growth. Teach them *your* need for the gospel.

Here's the main thing I want you to remember: when you sin against your family—and you will—you need to call a family meeting. You need to say, "I just did something that was sinful. I spoke to your mother in a way the Bible says I shouldn't. I want you to know that I've confessed this to the Lord, and he is faithful and just to forgive us our sins and cleanse us from all unrighteousness. But I want you to know what you just saw me do was sin, and I want you to forgive me. I make no excuses. It's not because I'm tired or something your mother did. It's not a habit I have. I'm prideful and sinful. I'm guilty. I'm sorry and I will make steps not to repeat this. The bottom line is this, kids: your dad is sinful and I need grace. I need Jesus Christ."

We as children sometimes look at our fathers and say "they can do no wrong." But we aren't perfect. So, from the very beginning, don't your children be let down when you mess up. Let them say, "I love my dad but I love my savior more. I love that champion. I love the one who forgives sinners. That's who I'm looking to. My dad isn't perfect but he's leaning on the one who is."

It's hypocritical to call your children to account for their sins but never admit your own. Their problem is that you are their father and Adam is your father. They need to see the gospel lived in order to live the gospel. If we aren't living the gospel before them, then why would we expect them to be remorseful or anything but manipulative? If you've presented yourself to your kids as always perfect or always with an excuse then, guess what, your kids will always fake being perfect or always have an excuse. But if you tell them that you are a sinner in need of the gospel, then they will see and by grace one day follow the model of going to Christ with their sins.

We need to discipline our kids to the glory of God. We also need to teach them mercy. "Judgment is without mercy to the one who shows no mercy. Mercy triumphs over judgement" James 2:13). We need to show our children the gospel.

Your children will either grow up in a performance-driven house or a grace-driven house. If they grow up in a performance-driven house, then they will either be hypocrites or rebels. If they grow up in a grace-driven house, they will be disciples who seek the grace of God.

In 50 years, when someone says to your child "tell me about your dad," there are going to be a lot of things they will say that will be embarrassing about your legacy. But more than anything else, the one thing you want them to be able to say is that their dad was a Christian—that he loved Jesus, obeyed Jesus, and prioritized the kingdom of God; that he was a humble man; and that when he was wrong he pointed us all to Jesus Christ.

Long after you're dead, that's the thing you want your children to say when they tell people about their dad.

ABOUT THE AUTHOR

Ed Moore is the senior pastor of North Shore Baptist Church in Bayside, New York.

Cultivate Humility

Erik
Raymond

Pride. Is there a more pregnant word in the English language? It's the mother-sin that gives birth to all others. We may sin in many different ways, but it's impossible to sin without being prideful. And as pastors, we are in ministry to fight against pride and to see an increase in humility. We long to see people come to know, follow, and reflect Jesus—the most humble person who ever lived. But we do this with the irritating, though persistent reminder that we are prideful. Like an itch in our throat in the middle of a sermon, we just can't clear our throat from the effects of pride.

If we're going to help our people, we pastors must cultivate humility. We need to grow in our Christlikeness to help others do the same. So how do we do it? Here are a few ways to cultivate humility in ministry.

1. DEPLOY THE ORDINARY.

If any of our church members asked us how to grow in humility, we know what we'd say. We'd start by telling them of their need to spend time with God in prayer and the Word. And rightly so.

Prayer is an expression of our weakness and need while also a declaration of God's strength and abundance. It clings to the God of steadfast love while acknowledging one's total dependence upon his grace. To fail to pray is to declare one's omnipotence, omniscience, and self-sufficiency. How much more prideful can we get than this? Likewise, when we read the Bible, we come face-to-face with the worth and works of God. We are reminded amid our spiritual amnesia of who God is and what he has said.

Neglecting these ordinary means of grace will hurt us. Like a physician who neglects his health, we can quickly write a suitable prescription for our friends while we languish in poor health. Pastors, we must not be like Naaman, who looked down upon the ordinary instructions to be made well (2 Kings 5:10–12). These prescriptions from the mouth of God are his means to make us well—and part of this means being humbled. Deploy the ordinary means of grace, and do not neglect them.

2. LOOK IN THE PROPER MIRROR.

I remember someone comparing ministry to looking into one of those mirrors at a carnival. Depending upon your perspective, you may be tall or short, fat or skinny. Your perspective changes as you move around. This is how it seems as we get feedback on our sermons, the health of the church, or really anything related to our ministry.

One may say the sermon was great—another implies it was a dud. One person tells you the church is so friendly—someone else says it's full of cliques. After a while, you don't know what you are seeing.

Pastor, how do you see your ministry? I've found that the answer to this question depends on the following perspectives: *how I view myself, how others see me*, and *how I think others see me*. Hopefully, you can see the folly in this.

My view of myself is rarely accurate. It's often inflated in my favor. My consideration of how others view me is also a distorted mirror. It can be inflated or deflated depending upon circumstances. The same is true for how *I think* others see me. If we let this question master us, then we become enslaved to the fear of man. We long for others' approval above everything else. We long to maintain a favorable perception.

This is deadly in the pulpit, but also in the counseling room and at the dinner table. It's a sinister trap that plays upon our pride.

What can we do about this? We need to look at another mirror. We need to ask the question, *How does God see me?*

I'm glad you asked. The Bible says we are loved before the foundation of the world (Ephesians 1:4–5). We are counted righteous in Christ (Romans 4:5). We are accepted in the beloved (Colossians 1:13–14).

Think about this, dear pastor: you are known by God to your very core and loved by God to the very end. You are united to Jesus and accepted in him. This is the mirror that eradicates pride and cultivates humility.

3. SMILE UNDER A FROWNING PROVIDENCE.

The trials of ministry are myriad. Pride runs through the church. Like a tornado in small Midwestern towns, it leaves only destruction in its wake. We see broken marriages, disunity among members and elders, apostasy, and a host of stomach-turning realities.

We also face our own spiritual, physical, relational, and economic trials. We are often laid low and driven to despair. We are bitter about the past, anxious about the future, and mired in self-pity about the present. In all of this, we forget a vital component of our faith: the providence of God. The Heidelberg Catechism defines providence this way:

> God's providence is his almighty and ever-present power, whereby, as with his hand, he still upholds heaven and earth and all creatures, and so governs them that leaf and blade, rain and drought, fruitful and barren years, food and drink, health and sickness, riches and poverty, indeed, all things, come to us not by chance but by his fatherly hand.

Everything comes to us, even the difficulty, as a result of God's fatherly hand. To forget this is to walk in pride. It's to accuse God of getting the past, present, and future wrong. We must never interpret the character of God in light of our circumstances. Instead, we are to interpret our circumstances in light of the character of God. God loves his people (1 John 3:1), works all things together for our good (Romans 8:28), and uses even the diffi-culties of life to strengthen our faith (James 1:2–4; 2 Corinthians 12:9–12; Hebrews 12:3–8). The old hymn rings true:

> Judge not the Lord by feeble sense,
> But trust Him for His grace;
> Behind a frowning providence
> He hides a smiling face.

We can smile under a frowning providence because we know God's heart toward us. This cultivates humility amid difficulty.

4. GIVE IT A REST.

"Why do you suppose you have to do all of this?"

That question lingered in the air like smoke from Gandalf's pipe. A wise and loving friend asked me this question as he deconstructed my schedule and motives for ministry. He saw some unhealthy patterns of work and rest. So he asked me, "Don't you believe that God is sovereign?"

This conversation popped the balloon of personal pride in ministry. I was sleeping very little, adding more hours to each week's work, and taking on more responsibilities. Texts and emails continued in the evening and early morning. Days off blended into days on. Rest became as common as topical sermons. And it was beginning to eat away at my health and happiness.

And do you want to know the tricky part? It was all under the guise of noble work: ministry. It couldn't be pride if it were ministry, right? It was. Sleeping is an expression of submission to God. It declares our humanity, our creatureliness, our dependence upon God and our agreement with his wisdom for our lives.

So pastor, take some time off. Give it a rest. Take one day off per week—at least. Use up your vacation days. Take advantage of holidays. Though it seemed counterintuitive at the time, it was true: my exhausting efforts for God had the scent of pride because I couldn't trust God enough to rest. Regardless of your theological convictions about the Sabbath, we can all agree that rest is God's good gift that we should steward well for his glory and our good (Psalm 127:2; James 1:17).

5. LOOK AT THE LORD JESUS.

There are certainly more ways to cultivate humility in ministry. As we pursue them, may we always remember the posture of humility we find in the gospel. May we always remember the Lord Jesus, the incarnated epitome of humility; the one who condescended to rescue and redeem us from our sin.

And as we consider Jesus, we see that the way up is the way down. The narrow road is paved with humility. May we pastors lead our people by walking that road, following our Master every step of the way (Philippians 2:5–11).

ABOUT THE AUTHOR

Erik Raymond is the senior pastor at Redeemer Fellowship Church in Metro Boston. He and his wife Christie have six children. He blogs at Ordinary Pastor. You can find him on Twitter at @erikraymond.

Patience: A Pastor's Superpower

Dan Miller

A *Dennis the Menace* comic strip by Hank Ketcham pictures young Dennis sitting at the kitchen table with paper and crayons. He has wadded up a piece of paper and pitches it to the ground. Busy with food preparation, his mother cocks her head to catch her son's exasperated outburst: "How come patience takes so LONG?" Indeed!

The church I serve as lead pastor has patiently welcomed my ministry among them for 30 years. Like any good marriage, love has played a leading role in our hard-won relationship. Patience has played a major supporting role in the outworking of that love. Pastoral patience—the capacity to invest sufficient time in the pursuit of kingdom outcomes without freaking out—is a vital virtue in the exercise of pastoral care.

What fool would claim to be an exemplar of pastoral patience? I sometimes wonder if 30 years of service to a single flock is more indicative of my unimaginative, head-down, plow-horse orientation to life than it is to patience. In any event, patience is a prime color on the palette of pastoral fidelity. Consider a few examples.

PATIENCE WITH PROSPERITY

"Prosperity" is a much-abused word I wish to redeem for the purpose at hand. By "prosperity" I speak narrowly of that stage in a church's life at which she attains relative financial stability and maturity. At this juncture, members of the church, as well as discerning members of churches in close fellowship, sense that your church has attained stable ground, is unified in purpose, and demonstrates substantial kingdom returns on her biblically calibrated ministry.

A sizeable majority of pastors are called to churches having yet to attain such a stage of spiritual prosperity. Pastors of church plants, revitalization efforts, and a host of other unexceptional congregations will begin their ministries in environments that are shaky at best, if not largely dysfunctional. Most of us assume leadership of churches tottering on wobbly legs.

It takes gutsy patience to stay the course week in and week out, year after year, while the milestone of healthy stability seems no closer on the horizon. Temptations to impatient "solutions" beset pastors along this grinding journey. Persevering patience keeps your hand on the plow when inquiries about the size of your congregation prove embarrassing—or when someone sees a picture of your church's building, hears the paltry figure of your missions budget, or wonders why you don't have more elders by now.

I accepted the call of a church with 10 families. We were squatters, meeting with no lease in the basement of a languishing retail mall. For the next 22 years, we labored in a string of inferior buildings. I'm well acquainted with the way pride assaults such plodding patience by waving tantalizing shortcuts to prosperity in your face. After all, I started pastoring in the heyday of the so-called church growth movement. Such shortcuts were well-packaged and widely marketed for immediate implementation. All one had to do, we were exhorted, was plug in. Or shove off. But the blueprint required multiple services practicing liturgical apartheid, entertainment evangelism, and the jettisoning of formal church membership, corrective discipline, and expository preaching. So I had to tell myself, "Patience, Dan. Tune out the noise. Serve the reigning Christ. Gently lead the flock to calibrate ministry to the New Testament pattern. Permit the seeds to germinate. Wait on Jesus."

Alongside the allure of unfaithful methods designed to manufacture rapid growth is the temptation to jump ship. Opportunities may arise for a younger pastor to lead a larger church or join a more prestigious ministry. God may indeed call a pastor to leave his flock, but impatience can render us so itchy to "do something bigger for God" we abandon our flock like a hireling. Patience is renowned for her counsel to stay the course. What God can do with me elsewhere, he can usually do with me right where I am.

PATIENCE WITH PEOPLE

Shepherds lead sheep and sheep are slow creatures—*really* slow creatures! They don't change or move quickly. By nature, they meander and mosey, hesitate and halt. Pastoral impatience with slow moving sheep is understandable. It is also lethal.

Pastoral discipleship is fueled by patience. Gossips slip up. Alcoholics and drug addicts relapse. The fearful find new reasons to fret. Marriages recover, then devolve. The unrepentant dig in their heels. The promiscuous return to their vomit. Critical complainers find fresh reasons to bellyache. The proud justify new reasons to uncase their trumpets. The spiritually weak keep stumbling, while spurning wise counsel on where to walk. Meanwhile, faithful pastors keep on loving all of them. Pastoral patience stokes our resolve to walk alongside sinners who move forward so slowly and backward so effortlessly.

Coupled with prayer, nothing inflames such patience with people like meditating on God's patience with me. He never ditches his covenantal love for me out of frustration. He remains unrelentingly loyal to me as his son—day after day, failure after failure, weakness stacked on weakness, ugliness oozing from my spirit. He never leaves me or forsakes me. For reasons that outstrip credulity, he just keeps loving me, loving me, loving me.

This God, this Lord of unrelenting grace, may call me to leave the church I shepherd. But he will never call me to quit on them. I've had days I wanted to quit on my church family. I have especially longed to quit on certain members of that family. On occasion, the desire grows strong enough to fantasize about ditching the few at the cost of the many. But in those selfish, shriveled-spirit moments, Christ's steadfast love for sinners compels repentance and refreshed patience with his sheep. "Keep loving them, loving them, loving them."

PATIENCE WITH
PREACHING
PATIENCE WITH PREACHING

Preparing exegetically and theologically accurate, humanly engaging, skillfully organized, well-illustrated, ably applied, zealously delivered sermons is exhausting. Some weeks, it's impossible! Composing quality sermons is akin—as someone once put it—to sculpting cement with a spoon. Delivering them with unction is akin to draining a battery. Persistent, patient endurance is essential if one proposes to faithfully feed God's Word to his flock for any length of time.

Early in my pastoral ministry I could only afford a single, desktop computer. The church needed my computer at the church office so I found myself finishing sermons late on Saturday nights while my wife was at home alone. It seemed no matter how hard I tried, I simply could not conquer the blackhole of sermon preparation in a timely manner. Week after week I headed home around midnight, sometimes later. One such evening I lost it. Frustration inflamed anger and I violently slammed my hand on the dashboard of my car. "How come sermons take so LONG!?"

Well, the purchase of my first

laptop solved much of this angst, and a repentant heart went some ways toward changing my perspective on sermon preparation. I love the study, love the discovery, love the spiritual nurture such labor yields. But consistently bringing sermons to delivery remains an unrelenting, sermon-by-sermon discipline. Fatigue, distraction, competing responsibilities, and lengthy sessions of deep concentration demand patient endurance. There are many rich rewards for such labor. There are no shortcuts. Pastor, it's supposed to be that hard. And God alone can give us the patience to do it effectively for the long haul.

PATIENCE WITH PRAYER

I want to be a "man of prayer." I'm not one. Some people think I am, but they are simply comparing me to themselves. I pray every day. Prayer is my life-breath as a Christian warrior (Eph. 6:18). I love to pray, most days. But I am nothing close to an exemplar of prayer.

Nonetheless, I've prayed long enough to know that a genuine prayer life requires patient endurance. Patience is required to keep investing seasons of time in prayer when the demands of life are screaming at you to get off your knees and "do something." Patience is required to pray for the same people day after day—often with no evident answer to your petitions. Patience is required to pray when we don't feel like praying, when doubt bedevils confidence in God's promises, when our souls have grown calloused and unimaginative, when we are tempted to genuflect before the specter of pastoral despair, when we simply run out of words.

In the parable of the persistent widow, Jesus taught us to pray without losing heart (Luke 18:1). Jesus knows our natural bent against importunity in prayer—our struggle to invest sufficient time before God's throne to secure kingdom victories in keeping with the King's promises. He calls us, then, to patient persistence in this mission.

While these four samples of pastoral patience constitute a collective imperative, they are no product of our own ingenuity. The virtue of pastoral patience is fruit only the outpoured Spirit of Christ can produce in us (Galatians 5:22–23). May we rejoice, then, to throw ourselves in dependence upon him for the persevering patience to finish well, by his grace, and for his glory.

ABOUT THE AUTHOR

Dan Miller is the senior pastor of Eden Baptist Church in Burnsville, Minnesota.

God's Servant Must Not Be Quarrelsome

GOOD PASTORS KNOW WHEN TO PICK A FIGHT BUT PREFER TO AVOID THEM

Kevin
DeYoung

The pastor has the difficult task of being a non-argumentative person who knows how to make good arguments. He must be valiant-for-truth and a peacemaker, a man who contends for the truth without being contentious. Or as the Apostle Paul puts it to Timothy, "The Lord's servant must not be quarrelsome but kind to everyone, able to teach, patiently enduring evil, correcting his opponents with gentleness" (2 Tim. 2:24–25a).

We must not misunderstand the injunction against being quarrelsome. Clearly, by both precept and example, Paul did not envision the ideal pastor as a nice, soft, somewhat passive, universally liked, vaguely spiritual chaplain. After all, in the very sentence in which he enjoins Timothy not to be quarrelsome, he also emphasizes that there is evil in the world and that the pastor must correct his opponents.

Not all controversy is bad. The pastoral epistles are full of warnings against false teachers (1 Tim. 6:3; 2 Tim. 2:17–18). At the heart of faithful shepherding is the ministry of exhortation and rebuke (Titus 1:9; 2:15). Doctrine is not the problem. Disagreement is not even the problem. There are hills to die on. There are fights to pick. Staying out of the fray is not always the better part of valor.

A TIME FOR PEACE

But often it is.

In Titus 3, Paul instructs pastors to avoid four kinds of fights: foolish controversies, genealogies, dissensions, and quarrels about the law (v. 9). We don't know exactly what Paul had in mind with each of these categories, but we can piece together a general outline.

- Foolish controversies involved irreverent silly myths (1 Tim. 4:7), wrangling about Jewish folklore (Titus 1:14), and contradictory accounts of so-called knowledge (1 Tim. 6:20).

- The prohibition against genealogies doesn't mean it's wrong to trace your family tree, but it is wrong if you are doing so to prove a point of pride or to speculate about your past (1 Tim. 1:4–6).

- Dissensions likely have to do with divisive persons who love questions more than answers (Titus 3:10–11).

- Finally, the quarrels about the law that must be avoided are the kind that "are unprofitable and worthless" (v. 9).

It is hard to read the pastoral epistles without noting two major exhortations for Paul's ministry apprentices: (1) the pastor must not be afraid of battles, and (2) he must not like them too much. Most ministers in the broadly Reformed tradition will believe strongly in guarding the good deposit of faith (2 Tim. 2:14). And rightly so. But too often we miss the equally important theme that the pastor who loves constant controversy is a pastor who is probably not loving his people well.

WHAT TO AVOID

The pastoral epistles constantly warn against an unhealthy hankering for quarrels (1 Tim. 1:4–6; 4:7; 6:4, 20; 2 Tim. 2:14, 16, 23; 4:4; Titus 1:14; 3:9–11). While we may not know precisely what the problems were at Ephesus and Crete, several key words and phrases give us a good idea of what to avoid. Foolish controversies involve "endless genealogies," "speculation," "babble," "vain discussion," debates that are "irreverent" and "silly," "unprofitable" discussions, and "quarrels about words." They are "worthless" at best, and at worst "lead people into more and more ungodliness."

We could summarize by saying that the quarrels we should avoid have one or more of these characteristics:

1. *There are no real answers.* That is, the controversy is entirely speculative. There is no possible way an answer can be reached—or, it's not even clear that those in the fight care to reach a conclusion.

2. *There is no real point.* Stupid quarrels produce more heat than light. They stir up envy, slander, and suspicion (1 Tim. 6:4). They are silly squabbles, wrangling about words when no important doctrinal issue is at stake (2 Tim. 2:14, 23).

3. *There is no real rest.* There are some pastors who only know how to function in wartime; they've never learned how to lead a people in peace. The pastor who enters every sermon, every elders meeting, and every internet kerfuffle with hand grenades strapped to his chest is a danger to himself and to others.

4. *The real winner is the "truth" teller, not the truth.* What all foolish controversies have in common is that the argument is less about truth and godliness and more about being hailed as a godly champion of truth. Before entering into polemics, we would do well to ask questions like:

- "Is my main motivation to impress my friends or to make God's Word look impressive?"
- "Do I want to annoy or embarrass my enemies or persuade them?"
- "If the truth wins out, do I care who gets the credit?"

When controversies puff up instead of build up, the Bible calls them "vain" or "irreverent." Once the battle is over, no one is closer to God or godliness. The church is not holier and happier. In foolish controversies, the end result is that you feel better about yourself and (you hope) others feel better about you.

To be sure, this is not the point of every controversy. "Once more unto the breach" is a necessary rallying cry for the gospel minister. The office of pastor is not for shepherds who want to keep their uniform clean. But that doesn't mean we should be the ones throwing the muck. Courage is required, quarrelsomeness is not.

ABOUT THE AUTHOR

Kevin DeYoung is the senior pastor of Christ Covenant in Matthews, North Carolina. You can find him on Twitter at @RevKevDeYoung.

Be Hospitable

When I was a senior in college, one of the pastors invited me to his house for lunch after church. He took me into his office and pulled books off the shelf one-by-one. He gave a little summary of what each one was about and why it was edifying. I thought it was strange at the time. Was he trying to impress me with his books? I really didn't care about his books. He might as well have showed me a slideshow of his family vacation.

But he knew what he was doing. He opened up his home to me. He fed me. He took an interest in me and cared about my spiritual walk. The books were simply his way of encouraging a young man to grow in Christ. Thirteen years later, that single act of hospitality remains prominent in my memory and I am thankful for it.

Pastors must be hospitable (1 Tim. 3:2; Titus 1:8). It's a necessary qualification. But why? Business men, politicians, CEOs, professors, and other leaders can all achieve great success in their industries without showing hospitality. So why is the practice of hospitality a prerequisite for the pastorate?

I can think of four reasons.

1. GENEROUS HOSPITALITY IS A REFLECTION OF GOD'S MAGNANIMITY TOWARD HIS PEOPLE.

Our basketball coach once asked us if we should play the game happy. We all stared at each other in silence. He told us with a scowl on his face why happiness on the court was not an option. As the season progressed, I realized that he was not a happy coach and we were not a happy team. Our disposition was a reflection of his leadership.

Pastors must be hospitable because the way we lead and love is a reflection of the God we serve. God is exceedingly generous. He acts hospitably towards his creatures. In Eden, God gladly gave Adam and Eve permission to eat from every tree of the garden, withholding only one for their greater good (Gen 2:16–17). When Adam and Eve disobeyed, God graciously clothed their nakedness (Gen 3:21). To Israel, God gave a bounty of manna from heaven (Exod. 16). To everyone, God gives the warmth of the sun (Matt. 5:45), rains from heaven, and fruitful seasons, satisfying the hearts of mankind with food and gladness (Acts 14:17). To those in Christ, God gives us a seat at his table, making us partakers of a family meal (Mk. 14:22–25; 1 Cor 10:17).

God's people are to reflect God's magnanimity in the way they treat others. Living under God's law, Israel was to represent God to the watching world with sacrificial, neighbor-loving acts of hospitality. They were to share their bread with the hungry, bring the homeless into their houses, and cover up the naked (Isa. 58:7). Jesus said that the same kind of compassionate hospitality—feeding the hungry, giving drink, welcoming, clothing the naked—would characterize his true disciples (Matt. 25:35–36).

All of God's people are to practice generous hospitality because God has made us after his likeness in true righteousness and holiness (Eph. 4:24). But pastors especially must be hospitable. In the list of pastoral qualifications described in Titus 1:7–8, Paul juxtaposes "hospitable" with "greedy for gain." Practicing hospitality is the antithesis of greed because it means gladly giving away time, energy, resources, and convenience for the good of others. Through hospitality, pastors manifest the kind of self-giving, servant-leadership exemplified by our Lord Jesus (Mk. 10:45; Phil. 2:4–11). He gave his life so that he could prepare a place for us in his Father's house (Jn. 14:2–3).

2. GENEROUS HOSPITALITY KEEPS THE FOCUS OF OUR WORK ON PEOPLE.

If the goal of pastoral ministry is to organize great programs, create effective marketing campaigns, manage facilities, build a brand, and construct a strong social media platform, then pastors don't need to be hospitable. But pastors are not in the business of organizational management. In fact, we're not in a business at all. Pastors are shepherds of people (1 Pet. 5:2). Our work is primarily people-work.

When a faithful shepherd loses one sheep, he doesn't immediately turn to a marketing campaign to get five more. He leaves the other ninety-nine to find the lost one (Matt. 18:12–13). God has entrusted pastors with the responsibility to care for the souls of each individual member of the flock (Heb. 13:17; Acts 20:28). Richard Baxter wrote,

> Doth not a careful shepherd look after every individual sheep? And a good schoolmaster after every individual scholar? And a good physician after every particular patient? And a good commander after every individual soldier? Why then should not the shepherds, the teachers, the physicians, the guides of the churches of Christ, take heed to every individual member of their charge?[4]

A pastor will not be able to spend equal amounts of time with every individual member, but through hospitality, pastors can personalize ministry to specific people in specific ways. In our living rooms and around our tables, we are able to share in the specific needs, burdens, struggles, and joys of the people God has entrusted to our care.

It's worth repeating: Our work is people-work. If we care about numbers more than individual persons, media to the unknown masses more than ministering to members, Twitter feeds more than feeding others, or building influence more than building re-

---

4 Richard Baxter, *The Reformed Pastor, 91.*

lationships, then hospitality will fall by the wayside. Pastors are to be hospitable because a spirit of hospitality rightly prioritizes the care of people in the work of ministry.

3. PRACTICING HOSPITALITY FOSTERS DISCIPLESHIP THROUGH EMULATION.

An older Christian couple's act of hospitality strengthened my marriage. After dinner, I watched the husband do the dishes and sweep the floor with a cheerful spirit. I felt convicted. Watching him forced me to ask myself if I was serving my wife in meaningful ways around the house. Unbeknownst to him, his example encouraged me toward becoming a better husband. It's clichéd but true: some of the best lessons in life are caught rather than taught.

Pastors are to be examples of Christian maturity worthy of emulation (1 Pet. 5:3). Paul told Timothy to "set the believers an example in speech, in conduct, in love, in faith, in purity" (1 Tim. 4:12). It's hard to set an example if we're only around people on Sunday mornings. We must invite them into our personal space. Through hospitality, we put our lives on display for others to see. We give church members (and others) the opportunity to see us follow Jesus in ordinary, everyday circumstances. Hospitality thus becomes a platform for discipleship as others see how we practice what we preach.

4. GOD CARES ABOUT OUR JOY.

Every time we were asked to do respite foster care, I hesitated. Respite care meant we had to take someone else's foster kids for a period of time while the foster parents were traveling. Accepting respite care meant accepting lots of noise, many interruptions, difficult children, a messy house, and more demands on my schedule.

But here's the reality: every time the foster children left our house, I was sad to see them go. By God's design, serving those who could never repay me enlarged my heart and gladdened my soul. Showing them hospitality allowed me to experience what Jesus meant when he said, "It is more blessed to give than to receive" (Acts 20:35).

God doesn't require pastors to be hospitable to burden us with another responsibility. God cares about our joy, and he knows true joy is found in self-forgetfulness and selfless service. "If you pour yourself out for the hungry and satisfy the desire of the afflicted, then shall your light rise in the darkness and your gloom be as the noon day" (Isa. 58:10).

Pastors, be hospitable. We shouldn't spend all of our time buried in books. Instead we should talk about those books with others, perhaps even over a meal. Simple acts of hospitality could leave impressions that last a lifetime.

ABOUT THE AUTHOR
Matt Emadi is the Lead Pastor of Crossroads Church in Sandy, UT.

Be Generous—Give People and Money

Paul Martin

A few days before "the day" arrived, I sat in my office and cried. We were about to do a great thing, a "gospel thing," and send away about 30 of our members and all their kids to plant a new work on the other side of the city. Our launch Sunday was days away and I had decided to preach on John 12:24: "Truly, truly, I say to you, unless a grain of wheat falls into the earth and dies, it remains alone; but if it dies, it bears much fruit."

The death I saw before my eyes was manifold. People I really loved were really leaving: an elder, some deacons, several ministry leaders, family members, and good friends. For the foreseeable future, they would have that rush of excitement of starting something new. The following Sunday, we would be left understaffed with a smaller budget and a whole lot of lonely. More than that, we would never be the same. The old version of us was gone.

Don't get me wrong, I was all for the plan. The whole church was. But there was a dark cloud on the horizon that Thursday afternoon.

John 12:25 Whoever loves his life loses it, and whoever hates his life in this world will keep it for eternal life.

Dying, losing, and hating sound almost romantic in the abstract. But now, here we were. We were about to risk pain and loss. But we were taking God at his Word. We wanted to be about "much fruit" and "eternal life" and the hope of being on the same page as our Savior.

John 12:26 If anyone serves me, he must follow me; and where I am, there will my servant be also. If anyone serves me, the Father will honor him.

So, we sought to be as generous with this group as we thought we could wisely be. There is no formula to these things. We promised (and delivered) salary and help and prayers and encouragement, but we also failed to think of a thousand other things we might have done to strengthen our friends in the Lord (see 1 Samuel 23:16). Still, we tried to do our best and take Paul's words to the Ephesian elders as our own: "In all things I have shown you that by working hard in this way we must help the weak and remember the words of the Lord Jesus, how he himself said, 'It is more blessed to give than to receive.'" (Acts 20:35)

"It's more blessed to give than to receive." How we wanted to live that out the best we could. I can tell you: Jesus didn't lie. Through the years, we've found that trying to be generous with our time, scant resources, people, space, and leaders has brought us the joy he promised.

I wonder sometimes if we get this mixed up. Sending away my faithful and capable associate pastor to the other side of the city was slug to the gut. It didn't feel good. I loved working with him! I still love him. Yet we could identify need in that part of our metropolis, and we all agreed it would be good to try and plant there. And I think without Jesus' instruction through Paul I would have been tempted to hang on to what we had, rather than attempt to do anything about that need. On the surface, keeping everything status quo, continuing to build our own church—that looked like the path to joy!

But Jesus tells us there is joy in generosity. In giving. In dying to our preferences and pleasures. In taking the way of the cross rather than the way of collection.

It would be a lie to say the joy was immediate, or even sustained. Not long after they left, our own church surged in attendees. Now we had fewer elders and deacons and more need. We were getting run down and did not realize the Lord had things yet to teach us about working in his strength.

John 15:5 I am the vine; you are the branches. Whoever abides in me and I in him, he it is that bears much fruit, for apart from me you can do nothing.

Ah, this deceptive heart! So quick to turn everything true upside-down. I thought our generosity would earn us some relaxation. Surely, this was where we would find our joy. But God had other plans.

I speak here mainly in the first person or on behalf of us as elders, but the entire membership was in on this. In fact, the reason I preached that sermon from John 12 was that I did not want them to be surprised by the death of our old church. Things were going to be different. Members had to give up friendships and co-laborers and "a way of doing church."

New leaders had to be born, new office holders needed to step up, and new ways of doing things had to take place. This required the church as a whole to be generous. Praise God they were.

And they remain so.

This spirit of generosity has (I hope and pray) settled into the DNA of our church. We buy books to give away, we hold a monthly pastors fellowship to encourage local ministers, we just this year sent another pastor down the road with another 30 of our members to help re-ignite a sister congregation. We have temporarily taken in the membership of still another local church for a season to help them navigate out of some difficult waters. I hope we are doing all these things with the cross in mind.

Jesus gave up his life for us. That thought should startle us. He was generous with his entire self, so when we can find spots to act with generosity, we are aligning ourselves with the very core of the gospel message. To hoard resources and stockpile people should feel foreign to followers of Christ. We ought to glory in giving!

I am thankful for one local church pastor I watched like a hawk in my college and seminary days. He plugged away at the same local church for a gazillion years and kept on planting, revitalizing, sending, and sowing long before it was hip. I once added up the total number of members of all the congregations his church had planted and realized,

if all these folks had stayed under his roof, he would have been the pastor of one of the largest churches in Los Angeles.

But he was different. He was all about giving people opportunity, raising up new leaders, and planting new churches. He was also one of the most joyful and content people I have ever met. I decided way back then I wanted to be like him. I saw something in his life that rang true. Generosity. It wasn't until writing this article that it dawned on me that he was the first person I ever heard preach John 12:24. No wonder he preached it with power. He had lived it.

All told, we have helped to plant three churches and strengthen two others over the course of the last twenty years. We ourselves were a plant that started with a whopping six people. All of these efforts cost us. They required us to give time and money and attention and prayers and people. They also required us to give up things that would have made for an easier life. So, in many ways, we look back on these years with wonder. How exactly did God allow us to do these things? I also wonder: what more could we have done if we had risked even more?

In Malachi God asks his people why they weren't being generous toward him: "Bring the full tithe into the storehouse, that there may be food in my house. And thereby put me to the test, says the LORD of hosts, if I will not open the windows of heaven for you and pour down for you a blessing until there is no more need. (3:10)"

Taking all the particulars of her covenant relationship into account, one cannot help but note how God loves generosity. He loves it so much that he will not allow himself to be outgiven. As Paul tells the Corinthians, "Whoever sows sparingly will also reap sparingly, and whoever sows bountifully will also reap bountifully. (2 Cor. 9:6)"

Perhaps it all boils down to whether or not we believe the call to discipleship that Jesus gave his followers:

> And do not seek what you are to eat and what you are to drink, nor be worried. For all the nations of the world seek after these things, and your Father knows that you need them. Instead, seek his kingdom, and these things will be added to you. Fear not, little flock, for it is your Father's good pleasure to give you the kingdom. Sell your possessions, and give to the needy. Provide yourselves with moneybags that do not grow old, with a treasure in the heavens that does not fail, where no thief approaches and no moth destroys. For where your treasure is, there will your heart be also. (Luke 12:29–34)

Pray to be a church with a generous heart.

ABOUT THE AUTHOR
Paul Martin is a pastor of Grace Fellowship Church in Toronto, Ontario.

Pursue Friendships with Other Pastors

PJ Tibayan

Like all Christians, pastors want to hear at the end of their life, "Well done, good and faithful servant! You were faithful over a few things; I will put you in charge of many things. Enter into the joy of your master" (Matt. 25:21). Faithfulness requires we develop Christian character and perseverance.

But faithfulness is hard. We pastors serve with joy but discouragement rears its ugly head. It isolates us from others, incites doubt and uncertainty, and entices us to throw in the towel. When we're not careful, this disappointment morphs from appropriate sadness or anger to despair and cynicism. The cynical heart then protects itself from potential pain and disappointment. But it also hinders faithfulness to Christ and his people.

THE GIFT OF FRIENDSHIP

It doesn't have to be this way. The Lord is good to us. He wants us to experience his goodness even in our biggest disappointments. So he gives us friends.

I've known loneliness as a pastor, both as a solo church planter in central Los Angeles and the pastor of a revitalization in Southwest L. A. County. I've repeatedly faced desperation, and the need for more strength than I possessed. Thankfully, God in his mercy gave me new and developing friendships with other pastors to keep my head straight as I bore the weight of divine accountability (Heb 13:17) in praying, preaching, overseeing, equipping, and modeling mature Christianity to my church family.

In his book *The Meaning of Marriage*, Tim Keller describes four elements of friendship that speak to the four needs that every human has, including pastors.[5] Friendship consists of *intentionality* since a friend "stays

---

5 Keller, Timothy. *The Meaning of Marriage: A Couple's Devotional,* (New York: Penguin Publishing Group, 2019), 152.

close" to you (Prov. 18:24). We need brothers who intentionally stay close to us, check in on us, pursue us, and desire to get an update on our lives. Second, friendship is *constant*, loving at all times, especially the difficult ones (Prov. 17:17). We need friends who love us at our worst—when we've sinned and failed, and others have turned away. Third, friendship requires *transparency* with open reproof and correction rather than flattery (Prov. 27:5–6). A pastor needs friends he can be vulnerable and open with, whom he can trust. Finally, good friendships have *sensitivity*, where they know how to empathize with our pain and rejoice in our victories (Prov. 25:20).

Pastors carry a heavy load. We need friends who are intentional, constant, transparent, and sensitive. We need fellow pastors in our church as well as pastors outside of our church who can empathize and support us. When we enjoy these friendships, we receive insight and encouragement. Furthermore, because Jesus said it is more blessed to give than receive, we find more joy in Christ when we give of ourselves to serve our pastor-friends. We need to regularly de-center ourselves by investing time into our pastor-friends—for *their* churches and for *God's* kingdom among the nations.

DEVELOPING SUCH RELATIONSHIPS

How can pastors develop these friendships? A few things come to mind.

1. Specifically initiate a specific relationship.

Call and text someone. Schedule a meal. Send a message. Write a letter. Reach out.

2. Resource them.

Find out how you can pray for and with them—and then take the time to actually pray together. Explore how you can serve them or help them think through issues. Ask them if they need any help with preaching. Follow up with them after conversations. Like Onesiphorus to Paul, we get to refresh pastors of Christ's church (2 Tim. 1:16-–18).

3. Receive help and support from them.

Why? Because you need their help. If you don't think you do, it's probably because you have subconsciously concluded you are no longer desperate, pitiful, poor, blind, and naked (Rev. 3:17), and that Christ would not supply insight, value, or strength to you *through your pastor friend* (Rev. 3:18).

You need to feel and express your neediness to Christ first, and then to his undershepherds. Furthermore, you need to give them the opportunity to help their fellow pastor by letting them help you. I'm not saying you need to pretend to need a friend's help the way a dad lets his 4-year-old son help him shovel dirt. When you have genuine needs (and you *always* do), let your pastor-friends hear it and serve you by meeting it if they can.

My main suggestion to you is this: Develop new friendships this month with other pastors—or deepen the friendships that already exist. If that seems too daunting, set aside an hour this week to ask God to give you new and deeper friendships and to help you reach out to a fellow pastor.

CONCLUSION

If you deprive yourself of God's gift of pastor-friends, you might find yourself increasingly isolated and discouraged. You might fall into a small-mindedness that ultimately leaves you less faithful to your church family. But if you develop and deepen your pastor-friendships, your soul and your ministry will be strengthened—and your church, other churches, and God's kingdom will be advanced.

Dear brothers, by God's many graces in general and the pastor-friends he gives us in particular, let's keep doing well as good and faithful servants. For soon we will enter into the joy of our master.

ABOUT THE AUTHOR

P. J. Tibayan serves as pastor of Bethany Baptist Church in Bellflower, California. He is married with five children and is currently pursuing a DMin from Southern Seminary.

Recalibrating Sources of Encouragement

HOW MY SOURCES OF JOY HAVE CHANGED 10 YEARS INTO MINISTRY

Mark
Redfern

For the last several years, I've attended a monthly gathering of pastors in my area. It's interesting to hear (and overhear) the questions we commonly ask each other. Those questions often focus on Sunday worship attendance, budget, or remodeling and construction projects. From those conversations it appears that pragmatic church success metrics (bodies, budgets, and buildings) are alive and well.

Of course, I'm not suggesting that those measures are inherently bad or unimportant. People matter. Money matters. Space matters. But those aren't the ultimate or primary measures of a church's success. Neither should they serve as foundations for joy in the ministry.

In my decade of pastoring, I've undergone a shift in the sources of my joy. Perhaps I've had the naiveté of youth beaten out of me by the realities of pastoral labor. Have I grown jaded? I don't think so. In fact, far from growing cynical, I think I've grown more joyful.

As a young pastor, I didn't necessarily root my ministerial happiness in bodies, budgets, and buildings, but I often tethered it to externally verifiable criteria. I drank from the cisterns of productivity. I hoped for happiness in achievement. I was always looking for the elusive joy around the next big vision or ministry initiative: the next sermon series, the next membership class, the next baptismal service, the next discipleship group, the next book study, or the next missions project.

I did this so much that I failed to see the grace-produced gospel-fruit growing right in front of me.

- The reconciled marriage between two church members.
- The forgiveness asked for and freely given by two church members after the Lord's Supper.
- The grace given to two deacons after the death of their young sons.
- The consistent faithful plodding of nursery workers and Sunday School teachers.
- The church member initiating a discipling relationship with a new Christian.

I used to feel more joy over affirmation from public displays of gifting than observation of private acts of faithfulness. But now I'm far more encouraged by just watching a faithful deacon mow our church property than a compliment after a sermon, though those are sweet gifts of grace as well.

Here are five ways my sources of joy in the ministry have changed over the past ten years.

1. MY PACE: FROM FAST TO SLOW

First, my pace has changed. Early on, life was all about how much I could get done. I took joy in accomplishment. I was simultaneously completing two masters degrees while holding down a full-time teaching job and serving as a bi-vocational pastor. My pace was relentless.

Then, something happened: we added more children to our family.

It's amazing how much having kids teaches you about ministry. Having children forced me to slow down. Parenting is a long work. And parenting is a great picture of pastoral ministry. Paul viewed it that way himself (1 Thess. 2:7–12) and emphasized leadership in the home as paradigmatic for leadership in the church (1 Tim. 3:4–5, Titus 1:6).

2. MY PATTERN: FROM ORGANIZATION TO FAMILY

I have some administrative gifting. I would have done well in some sort of middle management role. I have always had a mind for organization and structure. In the early years of ministry, I leveraged that gifting (I hope) for the betterment of our church. But, much of my joy in ministry was grounded in (to use a metaphor that Colin Marshall and Tony Payne have popularized) "building the trellis."

Then, something happened: I began to understand that the trellis exists to serve the vine.

As I began to process this ministry mind-shift, I started viewing the church more relationally. I went from leading an organization to loving a family. Now certainly, the church is an organization. Administration is a vital spiritual gift and an area of ministry I actually enjoy. But

it's also an organism. The organization is meant to serve the organism. As Scotty Smith frequently says, our "to-love list" should always supersede our "to-do list."

3. MY POSTURE: FROM STRENGTH TO WEAKNESS

I went from a bi-vocational pastor to a full-time pastor in the middle of 2014. With ten years of teaching in the rear-view mirror, I was ready to run, full steam ahead, into pastoral ministry.

Then, something happened: I had a car accident and broke my hip and femur.

Just as I was ready to plunge into ministry, the Lord laid me aside with a debilitating injury. I had surgery and months of rehab before I was able to preach again. And, when I did, I had to hobble onto the stage—at first with a walker—to open the Scriptures. If I'm honest, it was humiliating.

But it shouldn't have been. My physical posture in those days reflected my spiritual need all of my days. I am weak.

More recently, I have been dealing with ongoing depression. Instead of seeing it as an impediment to ministry, I now see it as gift for ministry. Far from being something I should shun, I embrace it as a weakness through which Christ's power can be displayed (2 Cor. 12:9–10). I have grown to appreciate and be refreshed by the Apostle Paul's relentless vulnerability (2 Cor. 7:5–6).

4. MY POWER: FROM GRIT TO GRACE

Sadly, much of my early days in ministry were marked by a lot of grit. Now, to be sure, Scripture commends grit. Paul described his pastoral ministry in agonizing terms (Gal. 4:19). We're called to work hard. We toil. We strive. We labor.

But we do this in the strength that God supplies (1 Pet. 4:11). We do this by grace (1 Cor. 15:10). We do this with his energy powerfully working in us (Col. 1:28–29).

My power for ministry is not in myself. Of all the things God has called me to do, apart from him, I can accomplish none of them. God himself must act in all the work he calls me to do. "O Lord, you have indeed done for us all our works" (Isa. 26:12).

For me, this means that prayer and patience have taken on a much more prominent place in my pastoral labors.

5. MY PASSION: FROM MINISTRY TO GOD

It's safe to say that for quite a few years I loved the work of the Lord more than the Lord of the work. I had more passion for ministry than for God. Over the last few years, I have had to learn all over again the lesson Jesus' had to teach his disciples near the beginning of their ministries.

In Luke 10, the disciples returned from their mission trip with joy. "The seventy-two returned with joy, saying, 'Lord, even the demons are subject to us in your name!'" (Luke 10:17). Jesus responded by joining in their celebration, "I saw Satan fall like lightning from heaven" (Luke 10:18).

But then he issued this caution: "Nevertheless, do not rejoice in this, that the spirits are subject to you, but rejoice that your names are written in heaven" (Luke 10:20).

Man, what a party pooper! Or, is he?

Jesus knows where true satisfaction is found, and it's not ultimately found in what we do for God. It is found in what God has done for us. Ministry is so volatile. There are good days and bad days. Sometimes you're loved, and sometimes you're hated. But what God has done for us in Christ never changes. Our identity is forever changed. Our destiny is eternally secured. Brother-pastors, let's anchor our joy to God and what he has done for us.

As I gather with pastors in the future, I long to create a different atmosphere, one where the conversation becomes less about what we see, and more about the future we don't yet see but is nearer now than when we first believed.

ABOUT THE AUTHOR
Mark Redfern is a pastor of Heritage Baptist Church in Owensboro, KY.

Pastors, Watch Your Doctrine

Greg Wills

In times of social upheaval and protests against injustice is "watch your doctrine" the word pastors really need to hear?

I contend that it is. As social upheaval advances throughout the world, pastors will feel pressured to evaluate their teaching by its apparent usefulness according the needs of the hour. We will be tempted to evaluate our doctrine not on the basis of its truthfulness but its utility. We may even judge that the old doctrines are not useful because they no longer seem relevant to the needs of our hearers.

But no crisis can alter God's truth or God's commands. His word does not change or fade according to time and circumstance.

WATCH YOUR DOCTRINE

Sound doctrine" simply means the teachings of the Bible—the full concourse of truth that God revealed in the Scriptures. Sound doctrine includes not merely the precious realities about God, creation, redemption from sin, and Christ crucified and resurrected, it also includes Scripture's demands for repentance, personal holiness, and the rules established by Christ for his church.

Sound doctrine is thus fundamental to faithfulness. Orthodoxy and orthopraxy are never at odds. "Keep a close watch on yourself and on the teaching, and persist in them," Paul commanded Timothy, "for by so doing you will save both yourself and your hearers" (1 Tim. 4:16). Life and doctrine are so inextricably connected that you cannot effectively watch the one without the other. They cannot be safely separated.

OPPOSE FALSE DOCTRINE

Your teaching must also oppose the false doctrines currently attracting your flock. False teaching is not just falsehood. It is rebellion against the God who spoke truly in his word. Sin always involves at bottom a distrust of God's truth. False teachers will always assail and twist true doctrine. False doctrine is the chief weapon of the enemy and the chief support of all idolatries ancient and modern.

The false teaching most dangerous to the church is not that which rejects Christianity, but that which affirms it while seeking to restore relevance and effectiveness to its preaching.

Liberalism pursued this agenda in the early 20th century and the result was devastating. Liberal Christians insisted Christianity was losing relevance by continuing to focus on the old doctrines, even as advances in modern science and historical research had rendered it rationally impossible to believe the Bible literally.

Liberal pastors and theologians sought to "rescue" Christianity, not by openly opposing the Bible's statements about creation, miracles, and regeneration, but by failing to mention them, or by suggesting that their real meaning was spiritual rather than literal.

In the end, the search for relevant doctrine did not rescue the church in its time of crisis, it only added to the crisis.

Pastors, be alert and oppose false doctrine firmly and lovingly.

TEACH THE WHOLE COUNSEL OF GOD

Your teaching must include those doctrines which you are tempted to omit because you suspect that it will not really help your members to teach them. To remain silent on matters where Scripture speaks, however, is to say that we do not trust God's truth to accomplish God's purposes. Refusing to speak what God speaks is rebellion founded on distrust. By refusing to speak where Scripture speaks we are essentially indicting the Holy Spirit for revealing something that harms rather than helps.

Rufus Burleson reminded his fellow Texas Baptist pastors in 1849 that watching their teaching meant preaching the difficult and unpopular doctrines of Scripture no less than the others:

> There are certain parts of 'the faith once delivered to the saints,' to which we fear too little prominence is given. Among them, we should mention total depravity, election, the divinity and constant agency of the Holy Spirit, regeneration, the necessity of a holy life, the design of baptism, and church government. The present crisis demands that we give special attention to, and guard with sleepless vigilance, these important points of doctrine.
>
> There are two reasons which may secretly restrain some from contending for sound doctrine: 1st. It will repel from our church those persons who hold loose and erroneous views of doctrine, and our numbers, and sometimes our wealth, will thereby be decreased. We grant that our numbers for a while will be lessened by adhering rigidly to the 'old landmarks,' but we are fully assured that our real strength will be greatly increased. By receiving into our church men of all creeds and no creeds, our increase for a few years may be rapid; but such a church would be only like Jonah's gourd—the worm of error would eat upon its vitals, 'as does a canker.' In the day of adversity, it will wither and die.
>
> 2nd. Contending for our doctrines will diminish our popularity, and exposes us to persecution. This we fear, has more influence, even upon Baptists, than we suppose. But, could our venerable fathers arise from the dead, or speak to us 'from under the altar,' (Rev. 6:9) what would be their language? What would be the words of the Waldenses—of a Roger Williams—an Obadiah Holmes—a John Bunyan? Should we not hear them exclaiming: 'For these principles, we suffered exile—the lash— the stake—the dungeon—and will you desert them for a little breath of popular applause?'"

Let your answer be: "No. Never." Some of God's truth may not be welcomed by your hearers. That must not deter you. Preach all that God has spoken. Do not judge the effectiveness of the word of God; let it judge you.

God requires pastors to preach his word because we trust him in all that he has spoken, not because we judge his word to be useful.

Brothers, watch your doctrine.

ABOUT THE AUTHOR
Gregory A. Wills is the Research Professor of Church History and Baptist Heritage Director of the B.H. Carroll Center for Baptist Heritage and Mission at Southwestern Seminary.

What "Able to Teach" Means and Doesn't Mean

Sam Emadi

"I just don't think Colin should be a lead pastor . . . you know, he's an INTJ." I was dumbfounded. I'd known Colin for years. He was a good preacher, sound theologically, he loved people, and he had proven grit. I couldn't imagine why my friend was expressing concern about him being a pastor, particularly on account of some pre-fabricated personality type.

I asked for clarification. My friend replied, "Well, he's a 4 and we know 4s struggle as lead pastors. They're more suited for administrative roles." Seeing my confusion, my friend explained what a "4" personality meant according to the enneagram and what it might say about someone's suitability for pastoral ministry.

I started to wonder: *what initials and numbers characterized my life and fitness for ministry?* I'd never taken an official personality exam, but a Facebook quiz once told me that I'm most like Charlie from *The West Wing* and BuzzFeed seems to think

that, among Disney Princesses, Cinderella and I would likely be BFFs. I'll let others decide how that ought to shape my ministry ambitions.

Sure, few of us would so confidently equate personality types with specific ministry roles. But at some level each of us is tempted to follow the world's logic when it comes to identifying future pastors and elders, to look at the outward appearance rather than the heart (1 Sam. 16:7). We can value gifts, charisma, and stage-presence over godliness, clarity, and sober-mindedness. Scripture, however, checks our worldly outlook, reminding us that God wants his church in careful hands, not necessarily charismatic ones. Each qualification for pastoral ministry in 1 Timothy 3 and Titus 1 focuses on character, not gifts.

Except for one.

Paul tells Timothy that elders must be "able to teach" (1 Tim. 3:2). He tells Titus that elders "must hold firm to the trustworthy word as taught, so that

he may be able to give instruction in sound doctrine and also to rebuke those who contradict it" (Titus 1:9).

The only particular gifting pastors must demonstrate is the ability to teach. But what exactly does this mean? Must pastors be able to captivate an audience? Must they have a good stage-presence? Are pastors just faithful Christians... with a few extra doses of charm and charisma? What does "able to teach" mean?

"ABLE TO TEACH" ISN'T PRIMARILY ABOUT RHETORICAL ABILITY

It's easy to assume "able to teach" must have something to do with preaching. Simply put, if you want to be an elder, you have to be able to preach. But equating able to teach with preaching is an *over*-reading of this qualification. After all, Paul doesn't mention preaching in this passage and neither he nor any other New Testament writer assumes that preaching is the only context in which teaching occurs. In fact, elsewhere in his writings Paul clearly refers to "teaching" that occurs in the church outside the preaching ministry (Rom. 15:14; Titus 2:3). Further, Paul also recognizes that, even though every elder should be able to teach, only certain elders within the church will have any significant, consistent public teaching ministries (1 Tim. 5:17).

So if "able to teach" doesn't necessarily mean "preaches great sermons," then what does it mean?

Looking at the same qualification in Titus 1, we find Paul further explaining that being "able to teach" looks like "holding firm the trustworthy word," instructing in "sound doctrine," and rebuking unbiblical ideas (Tit. 1:9). This focus on sound doctrine continues throughout the pastoral epistles. The elder must not teach "different doctrine" (1 Tim. 1:3) but should model and teach doctrine with the power to save his hearers (1 Tim. 4:16). He must rightly handle the word of truth (2 Tim 2:15), avoiding "irreverent babble" that "will lead people into more and more ungodliness" (2 Tim 2:16). His teaching should produce in his listeners "repentance" and "a knowledge of the truth" (2 Tim. 2:25).

In sum, Paul focuses more on the *content* and *result* of teaching than with its execution. "Able to teach" isn't simply the "gift of gab." You may be able to captivate a crowd, but if your teaching isn't true or isn't producing holiness, you're not "able to teach."

Paul's own ministry models these commitments. He never boasted in his eloquence. To the contrary, he pursued soundness over style, clarity over charisma: "For Christ did not send me to baptize but to preach the gospel, and not with words of eloquent wisdom, lest the cross of Christ be emptied of its power" (1 Cor. 1:17).

"ABLE TO TEACH" IS *A LITTLE BIT* ABOUT RHETORICAL ABILITY

"Able to teach" is mainly about doctrinal integrity, not rhetorical ability—but it is a little bit about rhetorical ability. After all, you have to *communicate* sound doctrine to teach it. Paul wants pastors who not only rightly divide the word but can explain it in a way that produces godliness (1 Tim. 4:16; 2 Tim. 2:25).

Thus, being able to teach means you can communicate sound doctrine in ways that profit the church. There is nothing in the context of the passage that suggests Paul has a particular teaching format in mind. The point is, whether in the pulpit, a Sunday School class, a small group, or even in one-on-one discipling, pastors and elders need to be able to use words to clarify, not cloud, the meaning of Scripture.

So, what does "able to teach" mean? Here's my one-sentence summary: "able to teach" means a person is able to faithfully explain and apply the Bible so that listeners grow in their knowledge of Scripture and sound doctrine in a way that produces love for God and neighbor.

A FEW PASTORAL REFLECTIONS ON "ABLE TO TEACH"

In light of the above, here are a few suggestions for how this unique pastoral qualification should shape both our ministry philosophy and our efforts to train pastors and elders.

First, Paul emphasizes godliness in leadership—we should do the same.

As already mentioned, "able to teach" is a unique pastoral qualification—it's the only one that focuses on gifting rather than character. Better an average preacher with impeccable character than a "gifted" preacher with questionable character. Pastors *must* be godly. After all, ordinary, unspectacular preaching won't ruin a ministry, but moral failure will.

If you're a church looking for a pastor or a pastor looking for more elders, don't assume the best candidate is the best preacher. Some men who look impressive in the pulpit act like pagans at home. Look beyond outward appearance to matters of the heart (1 Sam 16:7). Identify men who love their wives, serve their family, cultivate church unity, share the gospel, practice hospitality, and disciple others. Somewhere in that cohort of brothers, you'll find men who are also able to teach.

Second, Paul demands that pastors and elders be "able to teach," and pastors should expect nothing less of themselves or their fellow elders.

"Able to teach" may be the only "gifting" qualification for pastoral ministry, but that doesn't mean it's negotiable. Pastors, consider how you can cultivate this gift among the godly, mature men in your church. Hold a regular service/sermon review. Buy doctrinally sound books for your people. Give feedback on others' teaching and preaching. And be willing to give away teaching opportunities so others can grow and develop as teachers.

Whatever you choose to do in your context, find ways to encourage others to develop their gifts. Some in your congregation will be more naturally gifted than others, but you can, in fact, teach others how to teach. After

all, John Piper got a C- in his preaching class, but he seems to have turned out fine.

Third, the fact that "able to teach" focuses more on doctrinal integrity than rhetorical ability should remind us that the pastor's job is to shepherd sheep, not attract a crowd.

That's it. That's the reflection.

Finally, pastors, take heart if you're an average (even below average!) preacher. God doesn't require eloquence, but boldness and faithfulness.

Preaching and teaching is discouraging. It's spiritual warfare. I know more than one pastor who types out a fresh resignation letter each Monday, overwhelmed by his rhetorical inadequacies in the pulpit.

But if we're honest, every Christian would rather have a faithful preacher who occasionally mumbles words and gets

lost in his notes than a shallow, captivating one. My friend Matt Smethurst often reminds me that sermons are like meals; we don't remember most of them but we're only alive because we've consumed them. If the food supply chain collapsed, would you rather someone give you a hot dog on a paper plate every day or gourmet meal on fine China once a month? A man who is "able to teach" knows how to deliver nutritious meals to his people, even if not all of them taste great.

Remember pastor, God requires clarity, not cleverness; doctrinal fidelity, not rhetorical flourish. As others have said, others may be able to preach the gospel better, but they cannot preach a better gospel. You may not be eloquent or effective by the world's standards, but God may still consider you "able to teach."

ABOUT THE AUTHOR

Sam Emadi is a member of Third Avenue Baptist Church in Louisville, KY and serves as the Senior Editor at 9Marks.

Three Warnings for Those Who Preach the Word

Ken Mbugua

There are not many callings in this fallen world that surpass the privilege of preaching. God has ordained that preaching would cause the light of his glory to shine upon sin-darkened hearts. He regularly uses preaching to bring into submission at the feet of Christ the lies that have long enslaved his people's hearts and minds. And he desires that preaching would cause the knowledge of the holy to be advanced through the church.

In short, preaching is a high calling.

And yet, in and around the shadows of the pulpit, soul-damning dangers lurk. Men better than us have fallen prey to the pitfalls of the pulpit. In this article, I want to articulate three dangers that threaten my own soul as a preacher who is desirous to fulfill his ministry. I pray for myself and my readers that the One who is able to keep us from stumbling will preserve us in this high and holy calling.

1. WE CAN MISTAKE KNOWING THE TRUTH FOR TRUSTING IN THE TRUTH.

As expository preachers, it's our business to know God's Word. Ignorance has no place in the pulpit. Our task is to mine the truths of the Scriptures and proclaim them to our people with precision, persuasion, and passion. In a world where truth in the pulpit is sadly uncommon, many who listen to us come with the bare-minimum desire to be taught the truth plainly.

The danger, of course, is that there will be theologically sound preachers in hell. After all, "The demons also believe and tremble." It's easy to teach on the sovereignty of God while clinging to the idol of control. It's easy to preach on the glory of God while seeking our own glory. It's easy to flesh out justification by faith alone while finding our justification in our preaching of justification by faith alone. Indeed, "when I want to do what is good, evil is with me."

We must not be deceived: no one was ever cured by selling medicine. For us the insult, "physician, heal thyself" must humble us and constantly call us to be partakers of the same remedy we prescribe. Our first calling must not be to expository preaching but to believing in Jesus. Our weekly labor must be aimed at more than ascending our pulpits with manuscripts spelling out God's truth; we must aim for consciences cleansed by Christ's blood, hearts singing of his matchless love, and minds captivated by the greatness of our God.

We must grow in the habit of responding to our own sermons in faith and repentance before and after we descend our pulpits. The best example I have seen of this is from a faithful pastor from across town who would often, as he interacted with his people after his preaching, share with his members the part of the sermon that most impacted him. He was a good model to me of maintaining my place under the rule of God's Word as a preacher.

Brothers, don't be afraid that you will fail to impress your hearers. Be afraid of preparing a feast for your members while you go home, week after week, famished. Pray for the humility and faith that you need as a preacher to be first a partaker of the fruit of your study.

2. WE CAN CONFUSE THE FRUITFULNESS OF MY PREACHING MINISTRY WITH THE FRUIT OF THE SPIRIT IN ME.

I was made aware of this danger from a Tim Keller sermon. He preached it at Beeson Divinity School's 2016 graduation from a weird, miniature pulpit. I will be eternally grateful for the exposure of this subtle lie, for I doubt that the enemy has a more deceitful way with which to lure ministers of the Word to a place of complacency with sin. How many preachers, blinded by the success of their ministries, have ignored the warning signs of the Spirit and continued, full-steam ahead, to shipwreck their faith? All the while, they're cheered on by "their followers" and pridefully believing that the fruit of their ministry meant they were special and the rules that apply to mere Christians somehow could not apply to them. How quickly we forget that the same Judas that betrayed Jesus also cast out demons.

We minister in a day when giftedness in the pulpit is prized over godliness. There are few churches that will choose the godly but average preacher over the gifted but somewhat immature preacher. Churches today are more likely to rationalize the lack of evident godliness than they are to overlook the lack of exemplary preaching skills.

Brothers, this means we are called to fight the battle on two fronts. From within, we must fear God, knowing that he is no respecter of persons. On the outside, we must flee the temptation of finding solace in the judgment of our hearers. Let Paul's words to Timothy be our standard: "I solemnly charge you before God and Christ Jesus, who is going to judge the living and the dead, and because of his appearing and his kingdom: Proclaim the message."

If we see ourselves as men see us in our pulpits, then we will all the more be tempted to confuse our fruitfulness with the fruit of the Spirit. But if we keep our eyes on that Day, then we might be saved from a mortal lie and thereby qualified to lead to a life and ministry that both saves our souls and the souls of those who hear us.

3. WE CAN FORGET THAT THE END OF ALL THINGS—PREACHING INCLUDED—IS WORSHIP.

When I'm working on a difficult passage that's not yielding a main idea or a clear flow of thought, my prayers have more to do with asking God to keep his children from leaving church unfed. In these moments, my main aim can be reduced to finishing the message without saying anything heretical. These are noble aims, but they're not of utmost importance.

Often, my anxiety in preparation reveals that my striving is not for the glory of God. My fearfulness reveals my concern not that God will look bad, but rather that I will look bad if I do not come through. My downcast heart plopped on the front pew after the occasional dud does not grieve that God was not exalted; it's grieving that I was not amazing. What I need most at that point is not the convincing words of the saints to reassure me that I indeed looked amazing enough and thus be encouraged in my identity as a preacher— what I need most is a broken heart that repents of my attempts to stealing the glory that belongs to God alone

B. B Warfield said that "all true theology must lead to doxology." The Apostle Paul, in laying out an argument for Christ-centered preaching, ends the section with the admonition, "The one who boasts must boast in the Lord" (1 Corinthians 1:30). If my "Christ-centered preaching" is actually focused on my own glory, it will show up in the nature of my anxieties and joys. While I may have kept the letter of the "law"—preach Christ crucified—I've missed the spirit of it: "that the one who boasts might boast in the Lord." When preachers pervert the purpose of the gospel, which is to the glory of God alone, they are no different from prosperity gospel preachers who pervert the content of the gospel and turn men away from the glory of God.

Brothers, we were not made for glory. We know that the God who knows all our weaknesses has made perfect provision for us in the gospel that we preach. So let's bring our glory-seeking pride to the cross, for there is mercy there—yes, even for a sin so vile as this. Let the gospel we preach be the best weapon against prideful preaching. Let's preach to our souls and to the saints that nothing that we would ever be tempted to boast in—not even our Christ-centered preaching—is devoid of sin. But praise be to God, through the precious blood of Jesus both we and the offerings we bring have been made acceptable to him. So let's rejoice and give all praise to Jesus who died to save all kinds of people—preachers included.

By his mercy, may it never be said of us that after preaching to others we were found to be disqualified.

ABOUT THE AUTHOR

Ken Mbugua is a pastor of Emmanuel Baptist Church in Nairobi, Kenya. You can find him on Twitter at @kenmbugua.

Keep Studying

Evgeny
Bakhmutsky

When I took my final exams at university I was convinced my life would only get easier. "Well, now I will have a calm and measured life," I thought. How wrong I was! Between work, seminary, ministry, church, and family, life only became more hectic. Yet despite my ever-increasing workload, I began to realize that having degrees did not mean that I no longer needed to study. Instead, I found that continuing in ministry required me to do more focused studies than I did even during my formal education. In college and seminary I faced theoretical problems. In the church, I faced real-life challenges.

The need to study doesn't end with seminary. In fact, it's only just begun. A pastor needs to continue learning, especially for these three reasons.

1. STUDY FOR THE SAKE OF YOUR LIFE AND MINISTRY

The famous French scientist Louis Pasteur proved in the 19th century that there is no such thing as spontaneous self-generation. Nothing is born from itself. Therefore, if we want to develop in any sphere —from personal spiritual life to raising children—then we need to invest in that particular area. Growth won't "just happen."

If we want to continue growing, then we need to learn through books, podcasts, research, and conversations. Pastors, therefore, should cultivate habits that will help them learn and improve constantly. Going out for groceries? Turn on a helpful podcast. Going for a run? Listen to a sermon. When you find yourself in your car or at the gym, start a series of seminars, turn on an audio book, or repeat your memory verses.

More importantly, visit people in your congregation. Don't let all your learning be "distance learning." Ask questions that help you learn how others think. In doing so, you become a factory that collects, analyzes, and then applies new information in your life and ministry. In essence, you are part of an exciting quest to find useful information and wisdom in all areas of life.

It's hard to help others grow unless we ourselves are growing and developing spiritually. We do not consume content to simply pass it on. We pass it on through our lives as we grow closer to God and help others do the same. As Paul wrote:

> Until I come, devote yourself to the public reading of Scripture, to exhortation, to teaching. Do not neglect the gift you have, which was given you by prophecy when the council of elders laid their hands on you. Practice these things, immerse yourself in them, so that all may see your progress. Keep a close watch on yourself and on the teaching. Persist in this, for by so doing you will save both yourself and your hearers (1 Tim. 4:13–16)

Continuous study has always distinguished true ministers of

Christ. Paul himself shows us an example when, even while in prison nearing the end of his life, he still set aside time to study God's Word:

> When you come, bring the cloak that I left with Carpus at Troas, also the books, and above all the parchments. (2 Tim. 4:13)

2. STUDY FOR THE SAKE OF INSTRUCTING YOUR CHURCH

As pastors, we all have our favorite topics to research or discuss. We love a good hobby horse. But if we're not diligent in studying, we'll find that those issues are the only ones we feel comfortable discussing. If we're not learning anything new, then over time we may just repeat ourselves on an endless loop—preaching nearly identical sermons year after year. Failing to labor in study is one reason why some pastors change churches when their pre-prepared sermons end.

But our congregations need fresh, thoughtful, engaged meditations "with all wisdom" because our calling, as pastors is "to present everyone mature in Christ" (Col. 1:28). Like Paul confessed to the Ephesian elders, we must be able to tell our congregations "I did not shrink from declaring to you the whole counsel of God" (Acts 20:27).

Reading books, attending conferences, studying articles, and assiduous attention to Scripture will expand our arsenal of knowledge and wisdom. So will expositional preaching through different books from different genres. These are tools which the Holy Spirit will use to help us guide the flock entrusted to us.

3. STUDY FOR THE SAKE OF PREACHING TO UNBELIEVERS

It's possible to say the right things in an unintelligible way. People may come to a gathering with heartache, but if we're not careful, they may leave with a headache. That's why ministers of the gospel need to understand their audience. Discerning pastors will study their own culture. They'll understand unbelievers around them, which will help them clearly preach the gospel.

Let me explain what I mean. I am a pastor in Russia. During Perestroika, many Western missionaries came into the Soviet Union and told their hearers, "God loves you. Accept his love!" It's a biblical statement to be sure, but it was often unclear to their Soviet audience. After all, Russian culture focuses more on how to receive God's mercy, not his love, and how to avoid the deserved wrath of God for your sins. They should have said something different. For example, "God loves you, so he offers you the forgiveness of your sins!" This would have connected mercy and love for Russian hearers.

Gospel ministers should stay intellectually vibrant. They need to grow spiritually, knowing their Lord and Savior; they need to increase in knowledge and wisdom; and they need to strive to comprehend their world and its people. In essence, this is the fulfillment of the two Great Commandments— to love God and to love people!

ABOUT THE AUTHOR
Evgeny Bakhmutsky is the pastor of Russian Bible Church in Moscow, Russia.

Build Fences Around Your Flock

Joel Kurz

Wolves devour sheep. In my first few years as a pastor, I was struck by the Bible's call to guard and defend God's people from wolves. Fake shepherds, called "hired hands" by Jesus, don't stand up to wolves—particularly those "wearing sheep's clothing" (Matthew 7:15). In contrast to the Good Shepherd, Jesus tells us that these hired hands do not care for the sheep, and therefore "the wolf snatches them and scatters them" (John 10:12–13).

As undershepherds, we must faithfully serve Jesus' sheep in light of his coming and in view of the unfading crown of glory which we will receive on that day (1 Pet. 5:4). We must guard the sheep against wolves. For this reason, we must know how to build fences; that is, we must lead our church in practicing meaningful membership and discipline.

WOLVES, KEEP OUT!

Fences are good. Fences guard the spiritually vulnerable from attack. They maintain the purity of the church which displays the gospel to the lost world.

So how do we build them? How do we keep wolves out of the church?

1. Teach on the purity of the church and practice church membership.

First, preach God's purposes for the church. Explain and define the biblical reason for church membership. Keep your membership records up-to-date, and teach your people to regularly pray through your membership directory. In other words, lead your congregation to know who your church members are and distinguish them from regular attenders.

Tools such as a church covenant and statement of faith will clarify who belongs to the church and how membership changes our relationship to one another. Does your church have a statement of faith? Members must know it and agree with it. Is there a church covenant? Use it.

If it needs to be dusted off, dust it off! In our church, we ask members to sign both the statement of faith and church covenant as a way of saying, "I agree with these things and am submitting myself to relationships defined by these principles."

2. Interview each prospective member.

One of the first questions we ask each prospective member is: "What is the gospel?"

We want to make sure every member understands and believes the gospel. If it becomes clear they don't understand it, we immediately pause the interview and move the candidate into a class called "Christianity Explained."[6]

Before we finally bring new believers into membership, we ask the candidate to give their testimony. As they do, we listen not with an overly critical ear but for a credible profession of faith that includes the existence of spiritual

---

6 https://www.thegoodbook.com/christianity-explained

fruit. As best as we can discern, we only want to receive genuine believers into membership.

3. Put membership (including baptism and communion) into the hands of your church.

The gathered people of God are better suited to maintain the purity of the church than a few pastors sitting in a room by themselves. Let your congregation have the final word on who belongs to your local church. Explain the candidate's testimony to the church and receive any questions prior to affirming the individual as a member. At Spurgeon's Metropolitan Tabernacle, this process involved two interviews, one with a pastor and then a Q&A with the congregation before the congregational vote.[7] Such a practice isn't biblically mandated, but we need to press in on our congregation's responsibility to oversee one another's membership in the local church.

Additionally, churches should only baptize those coming into membership (with a few rare exceptions).[8] Baptism is how we enter into the visible, gathered church. Baptizing without belonging, therefore, confuses membership and creates two tiers in the church: the baptized and the members.

Similarly, the Lord's Supper itself should function as a "fence"—clarifying who is *inside* the church and who is *outside*. At the table, the *church* is put on display. Pastors should fence the table with our words, warning unbelievers not to eat and drink judgment on themselves.

SHEEP, EAT HERE!

In addition to guarding against wolves, membership fences allow the sheep to graze safely. They inform church members *who* they are responsible for and *who* is responsible for them.

But our sheep aren't safe if we've allowed false teachers to slip in among them. For example, if a member of your church condones homosexual practice, the church is less safe for sheep who struggle with same-sex attraction. If someone in your church is a racist, "one another" ministry has been compromised. When pastors build membership fences, sheep can safely graze and be nourished through others in the body.

ISN'T THIS EXCLUSIVE AND UNLOVING TO THE WORLD?

Isn't all this talk about building fences a little exclusive? Doesn't this turn the local church into a club only for elite, righteous people? No, because the entry into the church depends only on faith and repentance. All who come to these waters can drink freely without cost (Isa. 55:1). Building a fence around your church only excludes the unrepentant and guards the purity of the church.

The church should be a light to the world and a city set on a hill (Matthew 5:14). It should display the gospel to the world around us. Our goal is to model a city within a city, a kingdom within a kingdom. What the world needs is not a social club that looks like them. The world needs us to be Christians, to gather in our communities, and to shine our light.

---

7 https://www.spurgeon.org/resource-library/blog-entries/meaningful-membership-at-spurgeons-metropolitan-tabernacle

8 Philip's baptism of the Ethiopian Eunuch in Acts 8 certainly allows for this in a missionary setting where there is no local church present.

ABOUT THE AUTHOR
Joel Kurz is the lead pastor of The Garden Church in Baltimore, Maryland. You can find him on Twitter at @joelkurz.

Whacking the Wolves

Juan
Sanchez

I received a phone call one day from a local church planter. The gist of the conversation went something like this: "Hi Juan. I hope you're well. Look, I just met with a guy. He will either be a great future elder, or he's a wolf. I'm not sure which one, so I'm sending him your way."

I understood his unwillingness to take that gamble. The church was still in its infancy, so, as you can imagine, still fragile. As a more established church with processes to identify future elders, we were in a better position to withstand the possible destabilization of a lone wolf. Thankfully, that phone call was enough to alert us to be on guard.

We won't always receive such preemptive warnings. So, how may we confront the problem of wolves in the church? At times, we must protect the sheep by whacking the wolves with the shepherd's rod. Lest we be quick to whack them, though, let's take our cues on handling wolves from the apostle Paul.

PAY CAREFUL ATTENTION TO YOURSELVES (ACTS 20:28)

Wolves tend to emerge among those recognized as teachers in the church. Paul acknowledged as much when he warned the Ephesian elders that "from among your own selves will arise men speaking twisted things, to draw away disciples after them" (Acts 20:30). Sadly, by the time Paul wrote 1 and 2 Timothy, it appears his concerns had materialized (1 Tim. 1:3–7).

There are any number of reasons why wolves emerge: love of money (1 Tim. 6:2–10); doctrinal confusion leading either to legalism or license (1 Tim. 4:1–5); power to draw away disciples after themselves (Acts 20:30). Because every pastor faces these same temptations, Paul called the Ephesian elders to "pay careful attention to yourselves" (Acts 20:28).

If we are to protect the sheep from wolves, we must guard our own hearts and pay attention to our own doctrine (1 Tim. 4:16). The pattern in the New Testament of a plurality of elders in local congregations is both biblical and wise. It helps us guard one another's hearts and watch one another's doctrine.

Brothers, what steps are you taking to pay careful attention to yourselves?

PAY CAREFUL ATTENTION TO ALL THE FLOCK (ACTS 20:28)

We must also pay careful attention to the flock. That's the job! The Holy Spirit set us apart to care for (*shepherd*) God's church (Acts 20:28). While there are many ways in which we protect the flock from wolves, let me highlight just three: identify the sheep, identify the pastors, and identify the wolves.

One of the most important ways we protect the church from wolves is to identify the sheep. And one of the ways we can identify the sheep is through a meaningful membership process. Equally important, though, is identifying the pastors. After all, if wolves tend to emerge from teachers in the church, we must be careful about whom we present to the church as teachers and elders. Brothers, does your church have a process for identifying regenerate members? And does it have a process for identifying faithful men who are able to teach others also (2 Tim. 2:2)—a process that is biblical and careful, where elder candidates are observed over time (1 Tim. 5:19–25)?

BE ALERT (ACTS 20:31)

Even with such processes, though, wolves will try to sneak into the flock. Consequently, we must be alert. We must also equip the sheep to be alert by leading them to feed on the green pastures of God's Word as it shows the truth and beauty of Christ and his gospel (Acts 20:27, 31). Once sheep have tasted and seen that the Lord is good, they will not want to feed on the "twisted things" offered up by demonic wolves (Acts 20:30). A faithful expositional ministry will protect the flock from wolves both inside and outside the church.

As shepherds, it's also our responsibility to identify the wolves. Again, Paul is a helpful guide. Writing to Timothy, he encouraged him to be kind rather than quarrelsome, "correcting his opponents with gentleness" (2 Tim. 2:24–25). Paul knew that sometimes sheep can be ensnared by the devil and look like wolves (2 Tim. 2:26). So as not to shoot such sheep, Paul encouraged Timothy to confront opponents with hope for repentance (2 Tim. 2:25–26).

But not all repent, do they? So, to identify the dangerous opponents, Paul outlined some of their characteristics (2 Tim. 3:1–7). One key difference between ensnared sheep and dangerous wolves is that God grants sheep "repentance leading to a knowledge of the truth" (2 Tim. 2:25), whereas wolves are "always learning and never able to arrive at a knowledge of the truth" (2 Tim. 3:5, 7). Wolves are unteachable. They refuse to repent of their false doctrine. Paul warns, "avoid such people" (2 Tim. 3:5).

WHACK THE WOLVES OR AVOID SUCH PEOPLE (2 TIM. 3:5)!

I take Paul's charge to "avoid such people" to be an exhortation to excommunicate the wolves. After all, how do you avoid such people in the church? You remove them. That's what it means to whack the wolves.

Take Hymenaeus and Alexander. They "made shipwreck of their faith," so Paul handed them over to Satan "that they may not blaspheme" (1 Tim. 1:20). That's the language of church discipline (1 Cor. 5:5). Hymenaeus is again named in 2 Timothy 2:17, this time with Philetus. Invoking the language of Korah's rebellion, Paul exhorted Timothy to "depart from iniquity" (2 Tim. 2:19). That meant Timothy was to separate himself from these wolves so as not to get swept up in God's judgment of them.

Brothers, if we want to be useful vessels in God's house, we will cleanse ourselves by fleeing youthful passions and pursuing righteousness, faith, love, and peace (2 Tim. 2:20–22). And when we identify unrepentant, unteachable wolves in our midst, we are to protect the flock by separating the sheep from them through excommunication that they may be delivered to the realm of Satan as they await God's final judgment.

ABOUT THE AUTHOR

Juan Sanchez is the preaching pastor of High Pointe Baptist Church in Austin, Texas. You can find him on Twitter at @manorjuan.

Love Your Church More than Its Health

Jonathan Leeman

This one goes out to the doctrine guys. The guys with ecclesiological opinions. The pastors and elders who think the Bible addresses the practices and structures of the church.

Wait a second, I'm talking about myself, and all of us at 9Marks, and maybe you. I thank God for you, and I rejoice to consider myself a co-participant with you in working for Christ's kingdom.

Yet there's a temptation I have noticed that you and I are susceptible to: we can love our vision of what a church should be more than we love the people who comprise it. We can be like the unmarried man who loves *the idea* of a wife, but who marries a real woman and finds it harder to love *her* than the idea of her. Or like the mother who loves her dream of the perfect daughter more than the daughter herself.

This is an implicit danger for all of us who have learned much from God-given books and conferences and ministries about "healthy churches." We start loving the idea of a healthy church more than the church God has placed us in.

I remember overhearing a church elder complain about a family who let their unbaptized children receive the Lord's Supper when the plate of communion crackers was passed down their pew. What struck me was the elder's tone. It was frustrated and slightly contemptuous, as in, "How could they?! The fools!" But these people were untaught sheep. Of course they don't know better. And God had given them this elder not to complain about them, but to love them toward a better understanding. At that moment, it felt like this elder loved his vision of the biblical church more than he loved those individuals.

How easy it is to respond like this elder.

WHAT I AM NOT SAYING

I am not saying that we should love people and forget all about biblical health, as if the two things are separable. No, that would be to pit God's love and God's Word against one another. To love someone is to desire his or her good, and only God defines "the good." To love your church means, in part, to want it to grow toward everything that God defines as good. It's to want your church to grow in a biblical direction.

More simply, if you love your children, you want them to be healthy.

So what do I mean by saying we should love the church more than its health?

BACK TO THE GOSPEL

When Christ died for the church, he made it his own. He identified it with himself. He put his name on it. That's why persecuting the church is persecuting Christ (Acts 9:5), and why sinning against an individual Christian is sinning against Christ (1 Cor. 8:12; cf. 6:15). Individually and corporately, we represent him.

Think about what that means. It means that Christ has put his name on immature Christians, and Christians who speak too much at members' meetings, and Christians who wrongly give their unbaptized children communion, and Christians who love shallow praise songs. Christ has identified himself with Christians whose theology is underdeveloped and imperfect. Christ points to the Christians who wrongly oppose biblical leadership structures and the practice of church discipline and says, "They represent me. Sin against them and you sin against me!"

How wide, long, high, and deep Christ's love is! It covers a multitude of sins and embraces the sinner. Actually, it doesn't just embrace the sinner. It places the whole weight of Christ's own identity and glory on the sinner—"my name will rest on them, and my glory will be theirs."

We should always come back to the gospel, shouldn't we?

GIVE YOURSELF, PASTOR, NOT OF YOURSELF

One theologian helped me understand an important aspect of gospel love by distinguishing between *giving of yourself* and *giving yourself*. When I *give of myself* to you, I give you something that I possess like my wisdom, my joy, my goods, or my strengths generally. Of course, I don't really risk losing anything in the process, because I gain praise for such giving. Indeed, I can give all that I have, even my body to the flames, and have not love. When I *give myself*, however, I don't just give something that I have, I give my whole self. I identify my *self* with your *self*. I start giving attention to your very name and reputation because I view them as united to my own. Any glory that I might have becomes yours, and all the glory that you have is the glory that I most enjoy. It's mine, too!

This is how we should love one another within a church, because this is how Christ has loved us. We don't just embrace one another; we rest the weight of our identities upon one another. We share one another's glories and sorrows. "If one member suffers, all suffer together; if one member is honored, all rejoice together" (1 Cor. 12:26). We consider one another better than ourselves, in the same manner that Christ has done with us (Phil. 2:1–11). Indeed, we have taken on the same family name, and so we are now brothers and sisters (Matt. 12:50; Eph. 2:19; etc.). If you insult my brother, you insult me. If you defraud my sister, you defraud me. Nothing's business in the church. It's all personal because the gospel is personal. He died for *you*, Christian. He died for *me*. So that we might represent and look like *him*. (Yes, he remains the final focus of our love for one another, just as his love for us was given so that we might love the Father—the final focus of his love.) If all Christians should love like this, we who are pastors and elders most certainly should.

To say that we should love the church more than its health means this: we should love people because they belong to the gospel, not because they have kept the law of a healthy church, even though that law may be good and biblical. It means we should love them because of what Christ has done and declared, not because of what they do.

If you love your children, you want them to be healthy. But if you love your children, you love them whether they are healthy or not.

Certainly you can rejoice when a brother or sister grows in theological understanding. You rejoice in the greater unity of truth you now share (see 2 John 1). But your gospel love—your "Christ died for us *while* we were yet sinners" love—should extend no less to the brother who is theologically, ecclesiologically, even morally immature, because such love is based on Christ's perfection and truth, not the brother's.

Pastor, if your church is filled with weak believers, you should still identify yourself with them as if they were strong. Maybe you feel more "like-minded" (a popular phrase among the Reformed) with the mature brother who shares your theology. Fine. But if that theologically-minded brother asks you to share his contempt for a less theological or mature brother, say to him, "My son, you are always with me, and everything I have is yours. But we had to celebrate and be glad, because this brother of yours was dead and is alive again; he was lost and is found" (Luke 15:31–32).

Elder, love your flock like sons and daughters. Get into the bleachers of their lives and root for them on the days they make their free throws and on the days they trip running down the court. Own their laughter and their fears as if they belonged to you. Abide with their folly. Don't feel threatened when they speak disdainfully toward you. Return the curse with a blessing. Remember that extricating sin from the heart is a slow process, and they can't always help themselves. Be patient like the One who has been patient with you.

Or to use a different biblical metaphor, your love for your church should be a "for better or for worse, for richer or for poorer, in sickness and in health" sort of love, even if it's not a "till death do us part" sort of love.

Shouldn't it? Shouldn't you be committed to your church like you're committed to your own body, because that's how Christ loved you and me?

THIS IS HOW PAUL LOVED

This is how Paul loved the churches. He gave himself, not just of himself. He told the Philippians that they were his "joy and crown" (Phil. 4:1). He told the Thessalonians the same thing (1 Thess. 2:19–20).

Pastor, do you regard the recalcitrant and theologically naïve Christians in your church as your joy and crown? Do you identify yourself with them that much? Paul refers to the churches as his "boast" (2 Cor. 1:14; cf. 2 Thess. 1:4). Do you?

Paul told the Corinthians that they were his "children" and that he was their "father through the gospel" (1 Cor. 4:14–15). He felt the same way about the Galatians and Timothy and Titus (Gal. 4:19; 1 Tim. 1:2; Titus 1:4).

Elder, have you united your name and reputation to your church like a father does with his son?

How often do we hear words of love and longing from Paul! He opens wide his heart, and yearns for the churches to do the same (2 Cor. 6:12–13). He longs to see them and be with them (Rom. 1:11; Phil. 4:1; 1 Thess. 3:6; 2 Tim. 1:4). He "longs for them with the affection of Christ Jesus" (Phil. 1:8). And he knows that his own distress is for the churches' comfort and salvation, and his comfort is for their comfort (2 Cor. 1:6). Paul didn't give of himself to the churches, holding just a little back for himself, like Ananias and Sapphira did. He gave himself.

And Paul didn't love just the mature Christians this way. Read his letters, and you'll quickly remember how unhealthy many of these churches were!

May God's Spirit increase our love so that we can imitate Paul, as Paul imitates Christ.

ABOUT THE AUTHOR

Jonathan Leeman is the Editorial Director of 9Marks, and an elder at Cheverly Baptist Church in Cheverly, Maryland. You can find him on Twitter at @JonathanLeeman.

Preach, Pray, Love, and Stay

Mark Dever   Paul Alexander

When I was interviewing with Capitol Hill Baptist Church before they called me to be their pastor, someone asked me if I had a program or plan to implement for growth. Perhaps to this person's surprise (and perhaps to yours too!), I responded that I didn't really have any great plans or programs to implement. I was just armed with four P's—I would preach, pray, develop personal discipling relationships, and be patient. In other words, preach and pray; love and stay.

PREACH

Maybe even more surprising to some, I said that I was happy to see every aspect of my public ministry fail if it needed to... except for the preaching of God's Word. Now what kind of a thing is that for a pastoral candidate to say to a church? What I wanted to get across was that there's only one thing that's biblically necessary for building the church, and that's the preached Word of God. Others could do every other duty,

but only I was responsible and set apart by the congregation for the public teaching of God's Word. This would be the fountain of our spiritual life, both as individuals and as a congregation.

God's Word has always been his chosen instrument to create, convict, convert, and conform His people. From the very first announcement of the gospel in Genesis 3:15, to the initial word of promise to Abraham in Genesis 12:1–3, to His regulation of that promise by his Word in the Ten Commandments (Exod. 20), God gives life and health and holiness to His people through the agency of His Word. From the reforms under Josiah in 2 Kings 22–23, to the revival of God's work under Nehemiah and Ezra in Nehemiah 8–9, to that great vision of the Valley of Dry Bones in Ezekiel 37:1-14, where God breathes the life of his Spirit into his dead people through the preaching of His Word, God always sends his Word when he wants to renew life in his people and assemble them for his glory.

The way God works is through the agency of his Word. He even says as much in Isaiah 55:10–11:

> For as the rain and the snow come down from heaven, and do not return there without watering the earth and making it bear and sprout, and furnishing seed to the sower and bread to the eater; so will My word be which goes forth from My mouth; it will not return to Me empty, without *accomplishing* what I desire, and without succeeding in the matter for which I sent it (emphasis mine).

The New Testament witness to the primacy of God's Word in his method is just as conspicuous: "Man shall not live on bread alone, but on every word that proceeds out of the mouth of God" (Matt. 4:4). The Word sustains us: "In the beginning was the Word, and... in him was life... And the Word became flesh, and dwelt among us" (John 1:1, 4, 14). Jesus, the Word made flesh, is ultimate life incarnate: "The word of the

Lord was growing mightily and prevailing" (Acts 19:20; cf. 6:7; 12:20–24). The Word grows and fights: "And now I commend you to... the word of his grace, which is able to build you up and to give you the inheritance among all those who are sanctified" (Acts 20:32). The Word is what builds us up and preserves us: "For I am not ashamed of the gospel, for it is the power of God for salvation to everyone who believes" (Rom. 1:16; cf. 1 Cor. 1:18). The Gospel, God's clearest expression of His Word, is His effective power for salvation: "So faith comes from hearing, and hearing by the word of Christ" (Rom. 10:17). God's Word is that which creates faith: "[W]hen you received the word of God which you heard from us, you accepted it not as the word of men, but for what it really is, the word of God, which also performs its work in you who believe" (1 Thess. 2:13). The Word performs God's work in believers: "For the word of God is living and active and sharper than any two-edged sword, and piercing as far as the division of soul and spirit, of both joints and marrow, and able to judge the thoughts and intentions of the heart" (Heb. 4:12). God's Word convicts: "In the exercise of his will he brought us forth by the word of truth" (James 1:18). God's Word gives us new birth. James advises a little later, "in humility receive the word implanted, which is able to save your souls" (v. 21). The Word saves us. Peter also claims regenerating power for God's Word: "[F]or you have been born again not of seed which is perishable, but imperishable, that is, through the living and enduring word of God. . . . And this is the word which was preached to you" (1 Pet. 1:23, 25).

There is creating, conforming, life-giving power in God's Word! The Gospel is God's way of giving life to dead sinners—and to dead churches (Ezek. 37:1–14). He doesn't have another way. If we want to work for renewed life and health and holiness in our churches, then we must work for it according to God's revealed mode of operation. Otherwise we risk running in vain. God's Word is His supernatural power for accomplishing his supernatural work. That's why our eloquence, innovations, and programs are so much less important than we think; that's why we as pastors must give ourselves to preaching, not programs; and that's why we need to be teaching our congregations to value God's Word over programs. Preaching the content and intent of God's Word is what unleashes the power of God on the people of God, because God's power for building His people is in His Word, particularly as we find it in the Gospel (Rom. 1:16). God's Word builds His church. So preaching his Gospel is primary.

Prayer shows our dependence on God. It honors him as the source of all blessing, and it reminds us that converting individuals and growing churches are his works, not ours (1 Cor. 2:14–16; 3:6–7).

Jesus reassures us that if we abide in him, and his words abide in us, we can ask any- thing according to his will and know that he will give it to us (John 15:10, 16). What a promise! I fear it is so familiar to many of us that we are in danger of hearing it as trite. Yet we must hear it as that which rouses us from our sleepy prayerlessness and drives us joyfully to our knees.

What then should we pray for as we begin to work for the health and holiness of the church? (1) What more appropriate prayers could a pastor pray for the church he serves than the prayers of Paul for the churches he planted (Eph. 1:15–23; 3:16–21; Phil. 1:9–11; Col. 1:9–12; 2 Thess. 1:11–12)? Allow these prayers to be a starting point for praying Scripture more broadly and consistently. This is another way you can unleash the transforming power of the Gospel on the lives of church members. (2) Pray that your preaching of the Gospel would be faithful, accurate, and clear. (3) Pray for the increasing maturity of the congregation, that your local church would grow in corporate love, holiness, and sound doctrine, such that the testimony of the church in the community would be distinctively pure and attractive to unbelievers. (4) Pray for sinners to be converted and the church to be built up through your preaching of the Gospel. (5) Pray for opportunities for yourself and other church members to do personal evangelism.

One of the most practical things you can do for your own personal prayer life, and for the prayer lives of other church members, is to assemble a church membership directory (with pictures, if possible) so that everyone in the church can be praying through it a page a day. Our church's membership directory has about eighteen people on a normal page. We also have sections for members in the area who are unable to attend; members out of the area; one page for elders, deacons, deaconesses, officers, staff, and interns; a section that records the children of church members, supported seminarians, supported workers (like missionaries), and former staff and interns. We usually encourage people to pray through the page number that corresponds to the current day of the month (e.g., June 1, page 1; June 2, page 2, etc.).

Model for your congregation faithfulness in praying through the directory in your own devotional times, and publicly encourage them to make praying through the directory a daily habit. Your prayers for people don't have to be long—just biblical. Perhaps choose one or two phrases from Scripture to pray for them, and then pray a meaningful sentence or two from what you know is going on in their lives at present. Get to know the sheep in your flock well so that you can pray for them more particularly. And for those you don't yet know well, simply pray for them what you see in your daily Bible reading. Modeling this kind of prayer for others, and encouraging the congregation to join you, can be a powerful influence for growth in the church. It encourages selflessness in people's individual prayer lives, and one of the most important benefits is that it helps to cultivate a corporate culture of prayer that will gradually come to characterize your church as people are faithful to pray.

LOVE

One of the most biblical and valuable uses of your time as a pastor will be to cultivate personal discipling relationships, in which you are regularly meeting with a few people one-on-one to do them good spiritually. One idea is to invite people after the Sunday service to call you in order to set up a lunch appointment. Those who express interest by calling and having lunch will often be open to getting together again. As you get to know them, you might suggest a book for the two of you to read together and discuss on a weekly, every-other-week, or as-often-as-you- can basis. This often opens up other areas of the person's life for conversation, encouragement, correction, accountability, and prayer. Whether or not you tell these people that you are "discipling" them is immaterial. The goal is to get to know them, and to love them in a distinctively Christian way by doing them good spiritually. Initiate personal care and concern for others.

This practice of personal discipling is helpful on a number of fronts. It is obviously a good thing for the person being discipled, because he is getting biblical encouragement and advice from someone who may be a little farther along, both in terms of life stages and in terms of his walk with God. So in this way, discipling can function as another channel through which the Word can flow into the hearts of the members and be worked out in the context of a personal fellowship. It's good for the one who disciples as well, whether you are a paid pastor or a non-staff member, because it encourages you to think about discipling not as something that only super-Christians do, but as something that is part and parcel of your own discipleship to Christ. This is in large part why you as the pastor will be wise to publicly encourage members to get together for a meal during the week with an older or younger member and have spiritual conversations over books on Christian theology and living. Members need to know that spiritual maturity is not simply about their quiet times, but about their love for other believers, and their concrete expressions of that love. A healthy by-product of non-staff members discipling other members is that it promotes a growing culture of distinctively Christian community, in which people are loving one another not simply as the world loves, but as followers of Christ who are together seeking to understand and live out the implications of His Word for their lives. These kinds of relationships are conducive to both spiritual and numerical growth.

As a pastor, a healthy by-product of your personal discipling of other members is that it helps break down defensive resistance to your pastoral leadership. Change will always meet resistance. But as you open up your life to others, and as they begin to see that you are genuinely concerned for their spiritual welfare (2 Thess. 2:1-12), they will be more likely to see you as a caring friend, spiritual mentor, and godly leader; and less likely to misunderstand your gradual initiatives for biblical change as personal power grabs, self-centered ego trips, or overly critical negativism. Developing these kinds of relationships establishes their personal knowledge of you, which is helpful in nurturing personal trust of your character and motives, and in growing an appropriate level of confidence in your leadership among the congregation. It gradually breaks down the "we vs. him" barrier that sadly but often subtly stands between a wounded congregation and a new pastor, and is helpful in paving the way for biblical growth and change.

STAY

When I arrived at Capitol Hill Baptist, I waited three months before preaching my first Sunday morning sermon. I simply attended. I had asked for this time in conversations that were held before I arrived. When I explained my reasons, they agreed. It showed respect for the congregation, it gave me time to learn what they were accustomed to, and it showed them that I wasn't in a hurry to change everything. I realize not all of us have the luxury of waiting three months to preach after our arrival; but if it's possible, I'd recommend it.

The best way to lose your place of influence as a pastor is to be in a hurry, forcing radical (even if biblical) change before people are ready to follow you and own it. It would be wise for many of us to lower our expectations and extend our time horizons. Accomplishing healthy change in churches for the glory of God and the clarity of the Gospel does not happen in the first year after the new pastor arrives. God is working for eternity, and he has been working *from* eternity. He's not in a hurry, and we shouldn't be either. So it is wise to show care for the congregation and concern for the unity of the church by not running so far ahead of them that people start falling behind. Run at a pace that the congregation can keep.

Of course, there are some things you might need to change rather quickly. But as much as possible, do these things quietly and with an encouraging smile, not loudly and with a disapproving frown. We are indeed to "reprove, rebuke, exhort." But we are to do it "with great patience and instruction" (2 Tim. 4:2). Make sure the changes you want to implement are biblical (or at least prudent!); then patiently teach people about them from God's Word before you expect them to embrace the changes you're encouraging. This patient instruction is the biblical way to sow broad agreement with a biblical agenda among the flock of God. Once this broad agreement is sown, change is less likely to be divisive, and unity less prone to fracture. As you work for change, work also to extend genuine, Christian goodwill toward people. "The Lord's bond-servant must not be quarrelsome, but be kind to all, able to teach, patient when wronged, with gentleness correcting those who are in opposition, if perhaps God may grant them repentance leading to the knowledge of the truth" (2 Tim. 2:24–25). Make haste slowly... and kindly.

The key to displaying and actually having this kind of patience is to have a right perspective on time, eternity, and success.

(1) *Time.* Most of us think only about five or ten years down the road (if that). But patience in the pastorate requires thinking in terms of twenty, thirty, forty, or even fifty years of ministry. This puts all our difficulties into perspective. Are you in it with your congregation for the long haul—twenty, thirty, forty years—or are you figuring on "moving up the ladder" by taking a bigger church in five or ten years? Are you building a congregation, or a career? Stay with them. Keep teaching. Keep modeling. Keep leading. Keep loving.

If you're a young, aspiring pastor who has yet to receive from a church an external call to preach, choose wisely. No one can predict the future or see all possible outcomes. But it may be less than wise to accept a call from a church or location that you couldn't imagine staying with longer than a few years. Go where you can envision contentedly putting down roots for the rest of your life, and commit.

(2) *Eternity.* As pastors, one day we will all be held accountable by God for the way we led and fed His lambs (Heb. 13:17; James 3:1). All our ways are before him. He will know if we used the congregation sim- ply to build a career. He will know if we left them prematurely for our own convenience and benefit. He will know if we drove His sheep too hard. Shepherd the flock in a way that you won't be ashamed of on the Day of Accounting. "Do your work heartily, as for the Lord rather than for men, knowing that from the Lord you will receive the reward of the inheritance. It is the Lord Christ whom you serve. For he who does wrong will receive the consequences of the wrong which he has done, and that without partiality" (Col. 3:23–25).

(3) *Success.* If you define success in terms of size, your desire for numerical growth will probably outrun your patience with the congregation, and perhaps even your fidelity to biblical methods. Either your ministry among the people will be cut short (i.e., you'll be fired), or you will resort to methods that draw a crowd without preaching the true Gospel. You will trip over the hurdle of your own ambition. But if you define success in terms of faithfulness, then you are in a position to persevere, because you are released from the demand of immediately observable results, freeing you for faithfulness to the Gospel's message and methods, leaving numbers to the Lord. It seems ironic at first, but trading in size for faithfulness as the yardstick for success is often the path to legitimate numerical growth. God is happiest to entrust His flock to those shepherds who do things His way.

Confidence in the Christian ministry does not come from personal competence, charisma, or experience; nor does it come from having the right programs in place, or jumping on the bandwagon of the latest ministry fad. It doesn't even come from having the "right" graduate degree. Much like Joshua, our confidence is to be in the presence, power, and promises of God (Josh. 1:1-9). More specifically, confidence for becoming and being a pastor comes from depending on the power of the Spirit to make us adequate through the equipping ministry of Christ's Word. "Such confidence we have through Christ toward God. Not that we are adequate in ourselves to consider anything as coming from ourselves, but our adequacy is from God, who also made us adequate as servants of a new covenant, not of the letter but of the Spirit; for the letter kills, but the Spirit gives life" (2 Cor. 3:4-6). And how does the Spirit make us adequate? What instrument does he use? It's not a program. It's Christ's Word. "All Scripture is inspired by God and profitable for teaching, for reproof, for correction, for training in righteousness, [why?] so that the man of God may be adequate, equipped for every good work" (2 Tim. 3:16–17; cf. Jer. 1:9; Ezek. 2:1–7; 3:1–11). The one thing necessary is the power of Christ's Word. That's why preaching and prayer will always be paramount—no matter what fad tops the charts. Stake your ministry on the power of the Gospel (Rom. 1:16).

EDITOR'S NOTE

This article is a lightly edited reprint of chapter 1 of *The Deliberate Church: Building Your Ministry on the Gospel* (Crossway, 2005).

ABOUT THE AUTHORS

Mark Dever is the senior pastor of Capitol Hill Baptist Church in Washington, D. C., and the President of 9Marks. You can find him on Twitter at @MarkDever.
Paul Alexander is the Pastor of Grace Covenant Church of Fox Valley in Elgin, Illinois.

What to Remember When It's Going Well

Ray Ortlund

"**B**e ready in season and out of season" (2 Tim. 4:2).

Pastoral ministry is seasonal. We pastors inevitably experience both winter-like blasts of ice-cold resistance and spring-like bursts of fresh life and responsiveness. And these changes aren't always explainable in terms of our ministerial performance. Maybe the greatest pastor of all time, the apostle Paul himself, knew the full round of pastoral seasons.

However your ministry is going right now, you know to do this: "Be ready." That attitude of urgency and alertness and eagerness is always right. But a guarded self-interest or a cowardly passivity or a defeated resignation is always wrong. As Jim Elliot put it, "Wherever you are, be all there!" Or to quote Richard Baxter, "Whatever you do, let the people see that you are in good earnest."

When the ministry is going well and people are flocking in and being converted and set free, you will be helped by remembering these three things.

1. REMEMBER HOW YOU GOT HERE.

Not by good luck, nor by good works. The blessing of God is the blessing of *God*—by his grace, for his glory. Remember how Paul put it? "I know that through your prayers and the help of the Spirit of Jesus Christ this will turn out for my deliverance" (Phil. 1:19). The apostle knew how the blessing of God comes down. It's by bold prayer and the direct help of the Holy Spirit.

I remember a time, during the Jesus Movement of the late 1960s and 1970s, as we were being carried along by an out-gushing of divine blessing we'd never experienced before, a friend said to me, "Ray, you know why this is happening, don't you? It's because for years there were little old ladies in our churches praying for revival." Those hidden heroes never saw the answer to their prayers. But we did. When my friend pointed it out, a sense of gratitude and wonder filled my heart. I wanted to steward the blessing humbly. I didn't get myself there, and it didn't belong to me.

When the risen Christ is pleased to *pour out* newness of life on your church at levels you never dreamed could be real in this life, remember how it came down. You didn't cause it by your cleverness *or even by your faithfulness*. You entered into an inheritance Someone Else paid for, an inheritance other people prayed for, a season of blessing the Holy Spirit himself activated—and all that, *in spite of what you deserve*.

Remember to stay humble.

2. REMEMBER TO SAVOR THIS MOMENT.

When God takes up the work in his own hands and accomplishes in two weeks what would take us twenty years, and we find our churches caught up in his felt presence as never before, it would be wrong to stay grumpy and demanding. Whenever God blesses us in this life, his blessing is both real and imperfect—real because he is involved, and imperfect because *we* are involved. And the very flaws embedded in the blessing should move us to *more* wonder and *more* joy and *more* gratitude, not less. Francis Schaeffer taught us that if the only outcomes we're willing to accept are perfection or nothing, in this life we will get nothing every time. And we will deserve it.

Theologically serious men like us can fall into our own version of perfectionism. But of all men, we who believe strong doctrines of the fall of man and the grace of God should be the happiest, even when our churches *stay* messy. What stands out in our eyes is not the human mess but the divine grace in the midst of it all. Indeed, if God super-blesses our churches, the mess will pop up to the surface more obviously than ever. Good! It's because God is dealing with us. And that is when, by his same grace, we can apply gentle pastoral remedies to people's real problems more helpfully than ever before. What a privilege!

Ezra and Nehemiah wisely urged the people when they were experiencing eye-opening clarity about themselves: "This day is holy to the LORD your God; do not mourn or weep" (Neh. 8:9). In a season set apart as unusually holy by the heart-revealing power of the gospel—remember to counsel your people not to spiral down into miserable shame but to rise up in joyous praise to God! We are *so* evil, we can corrupt even a holy day by an unbelieving self-focus, terribly dishonoring to the finished work of Christ on the cross!

Don't allow yourself to think on a Sunday afternoon, "Yes, today's service was like another Pentecost. But you never know. It'll probably come crashing down to nothing this week." What defeatism! When the book of Acts says "there was much joy in that city" (Acts 8:8), it isn't saying, "And wasn't that stupid?" It is calling us to respond to Christ with our own "much joy." If you and I accept the authority of the book of Acts, then let's act like it.

Remember to stay thankful.

3. REMEMBER WHAT'S OUT AHEAD.

Hardship is coming. How could it be otherwise? "Man is born for trouble, as the sparks fly upward" (Job 5:7). But we're fine with that. *Suffering is our super-power.*

What did our risen Lord say to us? "My power is made perfect in weakness" (2 Cor. 12:9). In other words, the most perfect way his power is experienced and displayed is when we can offer him nothing but our need. Our "best case scenario" is not our dream ministry career but "weaknesses, insults, hardships, persecutions and calamities. For when I am weak, then I am strong" (2 Cor. 12:10).

When the ministry is going well, remember that tomorrow's setbacks and reversals will be bent around in God's mighty hands into yet *more* blessing. You will not see it all in this life. But if you will put your trust in the Lord for your ministry, he will ensure that your impact resonates on and on into future generations.

Remember to stay expendable.

ABOUT THE AUTHOR

Ray Ortlund is the lead pastor of Immanuel Nashville in Nashville, Tennessee. You can find him on Twitter at @rayortlund.

What to Remember When It's Going Poorly

Ray Ortlund

"**B**e ready in season and out of season" (2 Tim. 4:2).

Pastoral ministry is seasonal. I made this simple observation in my last article, "What to Remember When Pastoring Is Going Well." Briefly, we thought through together the seasons of ministerial abundance. But what about the hard times? What should we remember when tragedy overwhelms us, or when we lose our way in confusion, or when we seem unable to please anyone and the congregation is stiff and cold—or even walking out?

1. REMEMBER TO ACCEPT HARDSHIP AS ULTIMATELY FROM THE LORD HIMSELF.

If the people aren't responding well, maybe you're the reason. Maybe, without realizing it, you're doing something to put them off, sabotaging your ministry. It might *not* be you *at all*. But maybe?

"Who can discern his errors?" (Ps. 19:12), David asked. In verse 13 he speaks of "presumptuous sins"—proudly obstinate sins. But the "errors" in verse 12 are a matter of our obliviousness. We can offend our Lord and step on people with the best of intentions! So our loving Lord *allows* the negative impact of our errors to land on us. It hurts. But that shock and embarrassment—*it is of the Lord*. He is opening our eyes, so that next time we'll be more careful, more sensitive, more respectful. Let us therefore deeply accept our Lord's discipline and let our defenses down and have a good laugh at ourselves—and do some healthy changing.

We ministers, in accepting the Lord's call to gospel work, have planted our flag for his kingdom with profound sincerity of heart. But sincerity is not enough. Indeed, our earnest sincerity can, by its very nature, make us *feel* more virtuous than we really are. We need others to help us discern our irritating mannerisms and discourteous words and unconvincing emphases. It's like a guy with bad breath. Who will love him enough to tell him?

I believe that every man should be in regular conversation with other godly men, with this humble appeal as the agenda: "Brothers, help me see myself." Who wouldn't benefit from that? Who can be above it? Your dear wife will help you, of course. But she might be too biased in your favor. Let other men, whom you trust, help you too. The Lord himself will be in it all, honoring your humble openness. Brother, your ministry *can* become "acceptable to the saints" (Rom. 15:31).

Remember to stay teachable.

2. REMEMBER THAT YOU ARE FULLY EQUIPPED IN EVERY ESSENTIAL.

I love 1 Corinthians 2:1–5 where Paul rejoices in his ministry. He knows what he has going for him, even with his modest persona and rattled nerves. Moving through the sophisticated cultures of our world, as Paul did then, facing both passive indifference and bold rejection, what can you and I count on everywhere we go? Nothing less than "the testimony of God,... Jesus Christ and him crucified,... the demonstration of the Spirit and of power." What in all this world can compete with that?

Your church might be small in numbers, but you are mighty with divine power. You might be lowly in prestige, but you are exalted with Triune glories. You might be limited in programs, but you are immeasurable in eternal significance. Stop feeling sorry for yourself. Stop resenting that big church across the street. Your small church is fully equipped in every essential with the truth of the gospel and the power of the Spirit. Your small church might well become Ground Zero for the next worldwide awakening.

How wonderful to remember that, with God, you just never know what he might do next! Stay close to him. Keep "swinging for the fence." And the Lord will surprise you with encouragements and breakthroughs, as you give your all to him.

Remember to stay confident.

3. REMEMBER THAT YOUR RUGGED, CHEERFUL ENDURANCE WILL PREVAIL.

The power of faithfulness is so great, our Lord Himself claims it as one of his own glories: "the faithful God who keeps covenant and steadfast love" (Deut. 7:9). If our Lord doesn't resort to a quick-fix but works faithfully over the long-haul, can we resent walking that same path?

We don't like patient waiting. Amazon Prime is counting on us being impatient! But it is those who "wait on the Lord" who renew their strength (Isaiah 40:31). The medieval rabbi, David Kimchi, explained that that Hebrew word "wait" suggests stretching, lengthening, extending. So "waiting on the Lord" is not like resting in a hammock with a glass of iced tea; it's like holding a plank position until our coach tells us we're done. But that place of unresolved tension is spiritually creative and surprisingly refreshing. Our strength is renewed. So we fight on, and we *will* prevail, because the Lord *will* come through for us.

"We wait with patience" (Rom. 8:25). The early church understood that. Yes, they saw miracles. But look at Romans 16 and how Paul greets his friends: "They risked their necks,... he worked hard,... my fellow prisoners," and so forth. They were powerless. But they prevailed. How? They waited with patience and refused to quit. They believed God is in no hurry, so they were in no hurry. They believed God is in control, so they felt no need to be in control. They believed God is powerful, so they didn't get pushy. Bishop Cyprian wrote to his suffering people, "As servants and worshipers of God, let us show the patience that we learn from the heavenly teachings. For that virtue we have in common with God."

One final thought. The world is racing toward final judgment. But God is with us. All his promises are true, all his purposes successful. And now it's our turn, in our generation, to bear witness to his glory. How? Keep going, keep going, keep going, keep going, keep going. And when we've done that, *keep going!* And *that* is how we prevail.

Remember to stay faithful.

ABOUT THE AUTHOR
Ray Ortlund is the lead pastor of Immanuel Nashville in Nashville, Tennessee. You can find him on Twitter at @rayortlund.

Love Your Flock

Bob
Johnson

"If I speak in the tongues of men and of angels, but have not love, I am a noisy gong or a clanging cymbal" (1 Cor. 13:1).

How can a pastor demonstrate his love for his congregation? Of course we should preach good sermons, lead good services, provide good ministries, love our own families, and care about the integrity of our ministry. By doing all of these things, you may be tempted to think that your church knows that you love them. But if you are intentional about showing them and telling them, then over time you will teach your people how to love and some of them will teach you, too. Here are some of the ways that I seek to do that.

1. Make yourself available on Sunday.

Arrive early and be available to greet and talk with people—before the service starts and long after it is over. If you can, show up in the nursery, chil-

dren's classes, and other ministry areas in order to thank, encourage, pray for, and listen in to what is going on.

There are many times when I am peeking in on some of the classes that I hear a teacher say something that I can reference later on in a sermon, which reinforces what was taught and is hugely encouraging to that teacher. Tell them that you are available to talk with them, as many will "not want to bother you." Eventually, if you say it enough, they'll be convinced that you *really do* want to talk with them.

2. Ask for prayer requests, pray for them, and follow up.

We provide a prayer request tear-off tab in the bulletin that people can fill out every Sunday and drop in the offering plate or turn in.

3. Send birthday cards and anniversary cards.

Every year I write new birthday cards and anniversary cards

for the members. We print our own, and I sign them as being from my wife and me.

4. Send baby congratulations and sympathy cards.

5. Mark the dates of loss and let them know that you remember.

When a death occurs in a family that I know is a difficult loss, I will mark that on my calendar and the next year (and often many years after), I will text them or e-mail them on the anniversary of that day and let them know I am praying for them.

6. Visit them in the hospital.

7. Go to sporting events, plays, and other things your people are involved in.

8. Have people into your home and cook for them.

My wife is an incredible cook, but if I can make at least one dish for the people we are hosting, or contribute something to the meal that we are taking to a family, it is really appreciated. I've learned how to bake bread, make ice cream, be very handy with the grill, and even make special pancakes.

9. When invited, go to their homes and eat with them.

10. If a child draws you a picture, put it on your door so that you can pray for them.

11. Tell them you love them.
Of all of the things that I have done to express love to my congregation, the one thing that seems to be appreciated the most is when I simply tell them how much I love them. I do not do it every Sunday, but I really should. Some of my people have told me that this was the only time they have heard someone tell them there were loved in a very long time.

Of all the places where people should hear that they are loved, they should hear it in the church—especially from their pastor.

ABOUT THE AUTHOR
Bob Johnson is the senior pastor of Cornerstone Baptist Church in Roseville, Michigan.

Be Courageous! Don't Avoid Hard or Awkward Conversations

Andy Davis

Among the most esteemed professions in our culture are "first responders," people who courageously move *toward* dangers and disasters rather than the normal human reaction of running for their lives. I think here especially of firefighters who go into burning buildings and rescue people despite the heat and the imminent danger of a collapsing building. Now I don't imagine that secular society will ever see pastors with that kind of esteem, but I do believe that we pastors must see a significant aspect of our pastoral ministry in that light: moving *toward* pain, suffering, sorrow, and dysfunction. And given that pastors' tools are words, that means especially not avoiding the hard or awkward conversations with the people of our flocks.

When the little boy Samuel heard God speaking his name for the very first time, Eli had to tell him to say "Speak, Lord, for your servant is listening" (1 Sam. 3:9). Little did Samuel know that the Lord was calling him to ministry, and was testing him to see if he would speak a very challenging message of judgment to a man he loved dearly—Eli. But Samuel faithfully told Eli what God had told him despite the pain it would cause, thus beginning a lifetime of courageous proclamation of words from God.

Pastors must similarly follow the leading of the Holy Spirit to proclaim God's Word in its fullness, even when it's hard. Paul said he did not "shrink back" from fully proclaiming the Word in all its dimensions, even if it brought temporary pain to himself or his hearers (Acts 20:20, 27). Pastors can neither be people-pleasers on the one side, nor take pleasure in hurting people on the other. A loving courage for the sake of the final blessedness of the flock is the goal.

HAND OR AWKWARD SCENARIOS ABOUND

People are complex, and sin complexifies. In my almost twenty-five years of pastoral ministry, I have had many hard conversations, as well as many awkward ones. Hard conversations include confronting someone in a significant sin pattern as a first step in a painful church discipline process. I once had to deal with a man in an adulterous relationship who thought he was still acting in complete secrecy. He didn't know that his wife had hired a private investigator who obtained proof-positive of the affair. In front of two church leaders, I read him the account of Ananias and Sapphira lying to God from Acts 5 and said, "Sometimes we only get one chance to tell the truth." I asked him if he was involved in an adulterous relationship. He lied to me and the other two men. Amazingly, within a month he had been diagnosed with the cancer that took his life in less than a year. Thankfully, after some time he confessed and renounced the sin completely before he died. But I never forgot how scary the lessons of holiness were from that fateful moment. I and the other two men still shudder with the memory. Other hard conversations include rebuking an openly disdainful church member from a consistent pattern of challenging the elders publicly; comforting a family grieving over the sudden death of a family member by suicide; suspending a man from ministry because of abusing relationships with co-laborers.

The word "awkward" would be attached to far less severe situations. Here are some examples:

- telling someone that thinks he has the gift of teaching that he really doesn't;
- showing someone a blind spot in their sanctification, a pattern of sin that they clearly are not aware of;
- telling a young single man who is sweetly pursuing a young single woman in the church that she is not really interested in him and he needs to back off;
- conversely, telling a young single man that he should be moving ahead in a relationship when he is dragging his feet (One man once said to his discipler who was urging him to pursue a godly young woman in their church, "I guess I'm waiting for a 'ten.'" The discipler answered, "Brother let me be honest… you're about a 'seven'… maybe a 'six'!" Now that's an awkward moment!);
- working with a socially awkward person whose mannerisms are off-putting for everyone that knows him— body odor, strange laugh, talks too much, too "touchy-feely," painfully shy, etc.;
- dealing with an extremely needy person whose insecurities make him want to spend as much time with you as possible;
- winsomely evaluating a person's ministry performance in detail—leading in worship, preaching, public reading of Scripture, or organizing the men's retreat;
- asking forgiveness of a person when we are convicted that we have been unkind;
- pointing out a consistent pattern of procrastination or sloppy workmanship in a church member's ministry;
- any interaction of any kind in which a person's child is misbehaving and their parenting could be improved (people are *extremely* sensitive about their children!).

I could list many, many others! As it turns out, imperfect people interacting closely with other imperfect people creates a river of such moments.

FOUR BASIC EXHORTATIONS

1. Be humble.

Before you confront any other imperfect person about his sins or weaknesses, spend significant time in prayer humbling yourself. Remember that no such pattern ever exists in another person that couldn't easily exist in you. This is exactly what I think it means to remove the log from your own eye so that you will be able to see clearly enough to remove the speck from your brother's eye (Mt. 7:5).

2. Be gentle.

As we've just noted, Jesus likened the correction we do in other people's lives to dealing with their eyes. There is no more sensitive part of the body than the eye. The cornea has around 7000 nerve terminals per square millimeter—around 300 to 600 times the number found in the skin. So when you have a hard or awkward conversation, use extreme gentleness. In your courage, be tender-hearted. Let them see that your heart is for their final blessedness in eternity, and that any pain the encounter is producing is shared by both of you. Job 6:25 says, "How painful are honest words!" Keep that in mind as you speak.

3. Be truthful.

Make certain that the hard things you are saying are actually true. Whatever work you need to do to ascertain the truth, do it. And make sure that your words are saturated with biblical truth. Use the pertinent scriptures. Let the Word of God be "living and active, sharper than any double-edged sword" (Heb. 4:12). Let it do its clean, sharp work in the soul. Make certain that you are being clear about the topic and the counsel you are giving. They should have no doubt about what to do when you get done. In other words, don't be so "gentle" that they are confused what that conversation was all about.

4. Be hopeful.

Point them to the eternal hope in Christ, that God is at work in them to fit them for glory. If you are closing one door—perhaps to a ministry or a relationship—then tell them that God will open other doors. Give them eternal perspective, and remind them that God is working tenderly for their final perfection. Give them a strong sense of your abiding affection for them as a pastor, and how much you see the grace of God working in their lives.

ABOUT THE AUTHOR

Andy Davis is the pastor of First Baptist Church in Durham, North Carolina.

Pray for Your People

Ryan
Fullerton

If you've been called by God to be a pastor, then I'm sure you desire to pray for your people. Sadly, desire is never enough.

When our Lord asked his faithful inner circle of disciples "to remain here, and watch with me," I'm sure they had a desire to faithfully watch and pray with the One they loved. Unfortunately, that desire was not enough. Instead, they became memorable illustrations of a painful truth every pastor has experienced when it comes to prayer: "The spirit indeed is willing, but the flesh is weak" (Matt. 26:41). How many times have you made a fresh resolve to pray for your people only to find yourself fast asleep because your "eyes were heavy" (Matt. 26:43)?

The goal of this article is to fight back against our tired eyes with the prayer-invigorating truths of God's Word. I'm hoping these meditations will cause your soul to rise up with the apostolic cry, "We will devote ourselves to prayer" (Acts 6:4a).

To that end, I offer six biblical truths that I hope will jolt us out of our prayerless slumber.

1. NOT PRAYING FOR YOUR PEOPLE IS A SIN.

Prayerlessness is sin. We need to be honest about this. A pastor who fails to pray for his people is as unbiblical as a pastor who refuses to preach God's Word. One of the sweetest realities of being a Christian is that we're now "slaves of righteousness" (Rom. 6:18). Despite "desires of the flesh" pulling us towards sin (Gal. 5:16), believers still have an unceasing desire to do what is right. Because God has written his law on our minds and in our hearts (Jer. 31:33; Heb. 8:10), we therefore desire to love righteousness and hate wickedness (Psalm 45:7; Heb. 1:9). The Spirit never permits Christians to tolerate sin in their lives. Like the congregants they serve, pastors can never be happy tolerating prayerlessness in their lives because prayerlessness is sin.

The prophet Samuel made this abundantly clear when he promised the people of Israel that he'd pray for them saying, "far be it from me that I should sin against the LORD by failing to pray for you" (1 Sam. 12:23). Samuel recognized that a failure to pray for God's people was a sin against God. Samuel was a leader among God's people. How could he claim to care for them when he didn't bring their needs before Jehovah-Jireh, the One who alone could care for those needs? And how could Samuel claim to lead God's people if he didn't lead them to seek the Lord in prayer? To leave God's people un-prayed for is to leave them uncared for, unprovided for, and unled, "like sheep without a shepherd" (Matt. 9:36). As pastors, we're called to flee sin and to pursue righteousness. We must learn to flee the sin of prayerlessness and to put on the righteous and wonderful habit of praying for our people.

2. PRAYING FOR YOUR PEOPLE GLORIFIES GOD.

One of my favorite verses on prayer is Psalm 50:15: "And call upon me in the day of trouble; I will deliver you, and you shall glorify me."

Every day of trouble is a day we have the opportunity and privilege of glorifying God. In comforting the sick, discipling new converts, and counseling difficult situations, we can sometimes feel like we're being distracted from our true calling, but this is a mistake.

Each and every trouble that comes our way is an opportunity to honor God as we call upon him for help—and he does! When he answers our prayers and works in the lives of the people we're praying for, he gets the glory. When he comforts the sick or fixes the logistical issues we've been having, he gets the glory because he did the work.

We should follow the advice of John Newton (1725–1807) in one of his hymns:

> Come, my soul, thy suit prepare:
> Jesus loves to answer prayer;
> He himself has bid thee pray,
> Therefore will not say thee nay;
> Therefore will not say thee nay.
> Thou art coming to a King,
> Large petitions with thee bring;
> For his grace and power are such,
> None can ever ask too much;
> None can ever ask too much.

When we ask the Lord to work in the midst of our troubles, we give him the glory he deserves.

3. WE ARE CALLED TO IMITATE LEADERS WHO PRAY FOR THEIR PEOPLE.

Hebrews 13:7 tells us to think about our church leaders: "Remember your leaders, those who spoke to you the word of God. Consider the outcome of their way of life, and imitate their faith." If you survey great leaders of the Christian church, one thing they have in common is they were committed to prayer. We see this in the life of the Apostle Paul who told the Colossians that he and his partners in the ministry hadn't "ceased to pray for" them since the day they heard about them (Col. 1:9).

What an example of perseverance! Non-stop prayer since the first day he knew about the Colossian sheep. Consider that, brothers, and imitate this way of life. Consider also the example of Epaphras, "who is one of you and a servant of Christ Jesus," and whom Paul tells us was "always wrestling in prayer for you, that you may stand firm in all the will of God, mature and fully assured" (Col. 4:12). Remember the example of godly men like Paul and Epaphras, men of prayer.

4. PRAYING FOR YOUR PEOPLE REFLECTS THE PRIORITY OF NEW TESTAMENT CHURCHES.

The outpouring of the Holy Spirit at Pentecost was an answer to prayer. The earliest Christian leaders, along with just over 100 followers of Christ, were praying and waiting when God suddenly moved in power (Acts 1–2). The earliest Christians devoted themselves to "the prayers" (Acts 2:42), and as the church grew and the demands of leadership increased, church leaders realized they needed to reset their priorities (Acts 6). The neglect of some of the widows in the church had helped them realize they couldn't do everything.

But what *should* be their focus? Should they focus on benevolence or administration? These were good and spiritual options (Rom. 12:6–8), but the leaders of the early church knew something was better. Under the leadership of the Holy Spirit they proclaimed,

"It would not be right for us to neglect the ministry of the word of God in order to wait on tables. Brothers, choose seven men from among you who are known to be full of the Spirit and wisdom. We will turn this responsibility over to them and will give our attention to prayer and the ministry of the word" (Acts 6:2–4).

Did you notice what made the apostles' list of what to they had to do? The study and teaching of the Word and prayer. The corporate church couldn't leave the widows to starve, of course. But the leaders realized they would lose everything if they gave up on prayer. All the generosity required to care for the widows would have dried up if the leaders hadn't continued to dip their buckets into the well of God's mercy by praying for God's people. If we want to have New Testament ministries, then we must understand and practice New Testament prayer.

5. PRAYING FOR GOD'S PEOPLE WILL LEAD THEM TO CHANGE.

As pastors, we long to see our people grow in Christ-likeness. We prepare sermons because we believe in the life-changing power of the Bible. We set an example for the flock because we know people follow their leaders.

But do we pray? To be clear, we need counseling, preaching, and training opportunities. But all of these are useless without the power of God unleashed through prayer. The Apostle Paul saw prayer as a primary means of promoting the sanctification of God's people. This is why he prayed,

"Asking God to fill you with the knowledge of his will through all spiritual wisdom and understanding that the Spirit gives, so that you may live a life worthy of the Lord and please him in every way: bearing fruit in every good work, growing in the knowledge of God, being strengthened with all power according to his glorious might so that you may have great endurance and patience" (Col. 1:9–11).

Knowledge, wisdom, understanding, life change, fruit-bearing, strength, power, endurance, and patience—what more could you ask for! For the Apostle Paul, all of these came to God's people by prayer. And again, in the book of Philippians, Paul prays,

"That your love may abound more and more in knowledge and depth of insight, so that you may be able to discern what is best and may be pure and blameless until the day of Christ, filled with the fruit of righteousness that comes through Jesus Christ—to the glory and praise of God" (Phil. 1:9–11).

Love, knowledge, depth of insight, discernment, purity, blamelessness, the fruit of righteousness—to the praise and glory of God. Again, all of these blessings came through prayer. Do the congregations we serve manifest these characteristics? Perhaps they don't because we "do not ask" (James 4:2). Oh Lord, move us to pray!

6. PRAYER IS HOW ORDINARY MEN DO EXTRAORDINARY THINGS FOR GOD.

For years, the elders at my church have sought to be obedient to God's call to pray for the sick in accordance with James 5:14. Each time we gather with one of God's suffering saints to ask the Lord to heal them, I'm encouraged by a single verse in the book of James. James reminds us, "Elijah was a man just like us. He prayed earnestly that it would not rain, and it did not rain on the land for three and a half years" (James 5:17). I've always felt that it's a tender mercy of God to place this verse near the end of chapter 5.

Think about this. James has just told the sick to call the church elders to pray over a sick person in the hope they'll be healed. He seems to think healing won't come once in a blue moon, that it is something we should expect God to do in the ordinary life of the church. He writes, "The prayer offered in faith will make the sick person well; the Lord will raise him up." What a promise! The elders are asking God to do a miracle. James knows how the average pastor is going to think: "Me? I'm just an ordinary man!" James anticipates this objection by concluding the Elijah story: "Again he prayed, and the heavens gave rain, and the earth produced its crops" (James 5:17).

James is saying, "Look, elders, you're just like Elijah, the one God used to change the weather patterns for three and a half years. Surely God can use an average man like you to do extraordinary things." What an encouragement! We don't need to be extraordinary for God to do extraordinary things through our ministry. Instead, we should fully and joyfully embrace our ordinariness and fling ourselves onto the extraordinary promises of God.

Brothers, I hope these six reasons will shape your conscience and move your heart toward deeper passion and the resolve to pray. Give yourself to prayer for your people. Why not ask God to direct you to some fresh resolves for prayer right now? Let the fruit of obedience flow out of a mind that is transformed by God's Word (Rom 12:1-2). Prayer gives glory to God, follows the example of great men of the past, reflects the priority of the early Church, changes our people, and is used by God to allow ordinary men to do extraordinary things. May God help us to pray!

EDITOR'S NOTE:

This article is an adapted excerpt from *Pray for the Flock: Ministering God's Grace through Intercession* (Zondervan, 2015).

ABOUT THE AUTHOR

Ryan Fullerton is the senior pastor at Immanuel Baptist Church in Louisville, Kentucky. You can find him on Twitter at @RyanFullerton.

It's Not All About Preaching

WHY PASTORS NEED TO CARE
ABOUT ADMINISTRATION

Jamie
Dunlop

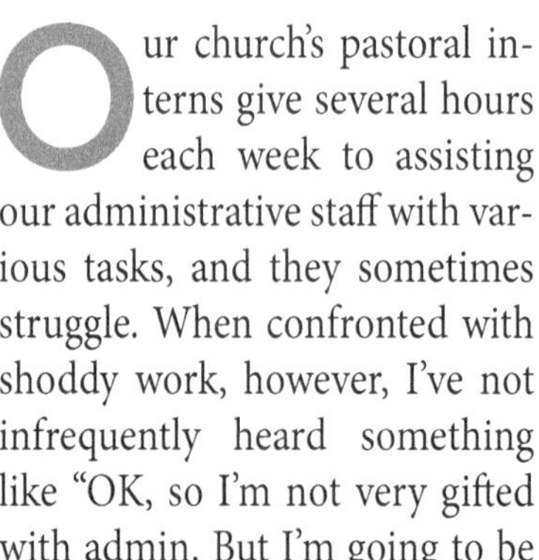

Our church's pastoral interns give several hours each week to assisting our administrative staff with various tasks, and they sometimes struggle. When confronted with shoddy work, however, I've not infrequently heard something like "OK, so I'm not very gifted with admin. But I'm going to be a pastor, right?"

Interesting question. Do pastors need to care about administration? The classic passage in the New Testament about the division between pastoral and administrative work is Acts 6:1–7. In this passage, the apostles tell the church to select deacons to organize care for widows so that they can "devote [themselves] to prayer and to the ministry of the Word." Yet in the Ephesian church, who assembled the list of eligible widows? Timothy, their pastor (1 Timothy 5). That example, plus the very fact that elders are often called "overseers" (Acts 20:28, 1 Tim. 3:1, Titus 1:7, etc.) would suggest that there is an administrative component to pa-

storing. To be sure, not every pastor is equally gifted with administration, just like not every pastor is equally gifted with counseling.

HOW PASTORS ARE INVOLVED IN ADMINISTRATION

So in what ways should pastors be involved in administration? Consider these four answers to that question.

1. Pastors set the tone for administration.

What are the goals for administration in your church? In some churches, administration is too efficiency-minded, crashing through pastoral concerns in its attempt to get things done. Elsewhere, sloppiness and carelessness is excused since it's "ministry," even though shoddy work defames Christ (Col. 3:23).

In the Jerusalem church, it was the apostles who defined the right goal for administration: to preserve the preaching of the Word and the unity of the church. Similarly, the pastors in

your church should also set the tone. They do this in the type of administrative staff they hire, in how much money the church sets aside for administrative tools, and in the goals they set for administrative volunteers. For example, when our church launches a new diaconal position (our deacons coordinate specific ministries, like a "deacon of childcare" or a "deacon of parking") an elder works with the deacon to determine what their goals are, often using Acts 6:1–7 as a guide.

2. Pastors identify pastoral implications of administrative tasks.

We see this point in 1 Timothy 5. Deacons may have administered the widows list but the more pastorally sensitive question of which widows qualified to be on that list was the pastor's job, at least by the time 1 Timothy 5 was written.

You can imagine many similar questions in your church. What's the right balance between building security and being open to visitors? How important is it that the congregation be visible to each other as you design your new meeting space? Should a divisive church member lead the ministry to international students? These questions involve tasks that are both largely administrative and highly pastoral.

That leads to two important questions: (1) as a pastor, are you familiar enough with the admin functions in your church to anticipate pastoral issues like these? And (2) do the staff and volunteers charged with managing these functions know to direct pastoral questions to a pastor?

3. Pastors oversee money in the church.

When Paul raised money to help the impoverished Christians in Judea, he also designed the accountability system for the money. In Paul's words, "We take this course so that no one should blame us about this generous gift that is being administered by us, for we aim at what is honorable not only in the Lord's sight but also in the sight of man" (2 Cor. 8:20–21). If this was worth the apostle Paul's time, then surely it's worth yours!

In particular, consider two ways that pastors should be involved in overseeing the use of money. First, pastors should ensure that someone they trust has reviewed the financial controls the church is using. After all, if something unethical happens, most in the congregation will assume that the buck stops with them (literally). Second, pastors should ensure that the money spent in the church budget is going to worthy causes.

4. Pastors communicate.

As a pastor, be on the lookout for administrative issues that have a pastoral dimension. Make sure you're the one speaking with the church about those things. I think there are three categories of administrative issues that warrant pastoral communication: (1) issues that affect your unity as a congregation (e.g. in some churches, the color of the carpet); (2) issues that touch on what makes a church a church (e.g. how many people should our new building seat); (3) issues that provide opportunities for pastoral instruction (e.g. what should we do about the recent slowdown in giving).

HOPE FOR ADMINISTRATIVELY-CHALLENGED PASTORS

If you're cringing right now, I can sympathize. I don't want this article to be one of those "and a pastor *also* has to be an expert in X and Y and Z!" articles. So let me leave you with two pieces of help if you feel you're administratively-challenged.

1. You can lean on others.

Especially in categories two and three above, these are things you need to ensure get done, but you don't need to be the one who does them. Those who assist you may have the title of deacon, or they may simply be administratively-minded and want to help. Either way, no matter your level of giftedness in this area, you should lean on others.

2. You can grow.

I've been impressed watching our pastoral interns over the years. Many of the "administratively-challenged" become quite capable administrators. How? Not mainly by reading books or by attending seminars, but simply by working to shepherd well because good shepherding will stretch some administrative muscles. Being an overseer *is* part of being a pastor, so we shouldn't be surprised that God's call on a man to pastor is often supplemented over time with gifts to administer.

ABOUT THE AUTHOR

Jamie Dunlop is an associate pastor of Capitol Hill Baptist Church in Washington, D. C. He is the author of Budgeting for a Healthy Church: Aligning Finances with Biblical Priorities for Ministry.

Pastor, Train Future Pastors

Garrett Kell

"Part of my responsibility is to send younger pastors into the land that I cannot go—the future."

I heard these words roughly ten years ago while serving as a pastoral intern under Mark Dever. Prior to that I'd been a pastor for seven years, but I had never even considered that faithfulness in gospel ministry meant investing in other pastors. I had struggled enough to *be a pastor*, let alone *help other pastors*.

Yet the more I studied Scripture and watched pastors I respected, I became convinced that pastors have the opportunity and responsibility to train other pastors. Not all pastors will do this work the same way, but every pastor should be devoted to the work.

Pastor training isn't just another item on our to-do-list; in one sense, it's central to our task. We want to protect and proclaim the gospel not only in our generation but also in the generations to come. We must train younger pastors to take the gospel to the land we cannot go.

THE BIBLICAL MODEL

As the gospel went forth from Jerusalem, sinners repented and churches were planted. The Lord called Paul and Barnabas to appoint "elders for them in every church, with prayer and fasting" (Acts 14:23). God charged them with the responsibility to recognize, train, and establish pastors to lead churches in carrying out the Great Commission.

But pastoral training wasn't reserved for the apostles. Consider Paul's instruction to Timothy: "What you have heard from me in the presence of many witnesses entrust to faithful men, who will be able to teach others also" (2 Tim. 2:2). Part of the way Timothy would "guard the good deposit" of the gospel (2 Tim. 1:14) was by training other men to faithfully teach it to others.

Paul gave a similar commission to Titus: "I left you in Crete, so that you might put what remained into order, and appoint elders in every town as I directed you" (Titus 1:5). The Apostle Peter seemed to expect younger men to be humbly training under experienced elders while they awaited their opportunity to serve in a similar capacity (1 Pt. 5:1–7).

When you search the Scriptures, you don't find seminaries training pastors, you find pastors training pastors. To be clear, seminaries have their place, but churches must not outsource the work of training gospel ministers. Seminaries should serve as a supplement to a church's pastoral training efforts, not a substitute for it.

PRACTICAL SUGGESTIONS

Being a pastor who trains pastors requires thoughtful leadership. What follows are five elements that go into developing a pastor-training ministry.

Reading these may feel daunting, but I encourage you to bring brothers along with what you're already doing as much as possible.

1. Entreat God desperately.

Jesus gives pastors to his church as a gift (Eph. 4:7–16; 1 Cor. 12). Unless he gives them and makes them grow, all of our training will be in vain (Ps. 127:1). So "pray earnestly to the Lord of the harvest to send out laborers into his harvest" (Matt. 9:38). Plead with God to raise up pastors for you to invest in. Pray that he'd raise up pastors to serve alongside you, pastors to send out from you, and pastors to one day replace you.

2. Equip men intentionally.

Though pastors are gifts, we also believe gifts from God are to be fanned into flame and not neglected (1 Tim. 4:14; 2 Tim. 1:6). To that end, create contexts in which future pastors can be trained. Whether you're investing in one brother or a whole crop of them, be intentional.

As we refine our pastoral training program we are continually asking: if I were an aspiring pastor, what would I want and need someone to teach me? What key books should be read? What skills need to be taught? What theological convictions must be formalized? What opportunities could be given? What feedback ought to be delivered?

Asking questions like these will help you develop an intentional approach to training aspiring pastors.

3. Exemplify faith vulnerably.

Many of the most valuable lessons I've learned in ministry came from watching other pastors in action. That's because training is caught as much as it is taught. Aspiring pastors should hear us say to them "imitate me as I imitate Christ" (1 Cor. 11:1; cf. 1 Cor. 4:6, 10:33; Phil. 3:17; 1 Thess. 1:6; 2 Thess. 3:9; Heb. 6:12). They should have a front row seat to "consider the outcome of [our] way of life and imitate [our] faith" (Heb. 13:7).

Something I always tell our pastoral interns is to observe me. Watch me serve well and watch me struggle. Watch me resist sin and watch me confess it. Watch me serve my family and watch me botch it. I tell them I'm an imperfect open book. As they observe me, there will be aspects of my life and ministry they will want to emulate and others they'll want to avoid.

4. Entrust opportunities plentifully.

Because ministry is not merely theoretical, training must include opportunities to serve. Creatively find ways to get aspiring pastors involved. Give them chances to pray, preach, teach, disciple, coun-

sel, lead meetings, visit members, perform funerals, etc. Resist the temptation to hold onto ministry opportunities as if they were really yours to begin with. Remember this is Jesus' kingdom and that he delights in us investing in the shepherds who care for his sheep.

5. Examine their work honestly.

One of the most important elements of pastoral training is to provide regular, honest, constructive feedback. If brothers serve without receiving godly encouragement and godly critique, they will not know how they need to grow. Study 1 Timothy 3:1–7 together and encourage evidences of grace while also pointing out areas where they need to grow. Give them opportunities to preach and then share feedback on what was edifying and what they could improve. Affirm their strengths and help them see where they need the strengths of others to complement them.

At times, this includes telling brothers when they aren't ready to be pastors. These are some of the most difficult conversations you may have. But if a brother isn't called or isn't ready, you serve them, their families, and other churches by telling them the truth. You should be gentle as you walk with them through this and also remember that John Mark ended up being useful after all (2 Tim. 4:11; cf. Acts 15:36–41).

I am eternally grateful to the pastors who loved me enough to take the time to help me cultivate my gifts—and to point out my flaws. If they had not spent time teaching me the Scriptures and modeling how to apply them, I know I would be of little help to those around me today.

Brother, I pray that as you read this list, it does not feel burdensome. God has called us to this work and my prayer for us is that we would "be strengthened by the grace that is in Christ Jesus" (2 Tim. 2:1). He delights in giving grace, so we have much hope!

ABOUT THE AUTHOR

Garrett Kell is the lead pastor of Del Ray Baptist Church in Alexandria, Virginia. You can find him on Twitter at @pastorjgkell.

Do the Work of an Evangelist

Jaime
Owens

We were two clergymen from different Christian traditions meeting for the first time. He stood on the sidewalk holding the leashes of his giant golden doodles. I sat on my front steps as we discussed missions and evangelism among evangelical churches. His perspective was a critique of mine: "We just live such good lives that *people come to us.*" It sounded like a nice piece of wisdom. Indeed, it was almost biblical (cf. 1 Pet 3:15). What struck me as odd was that last bit: people will *come to us.* Part of me wanted it to be true. Why not just be quiet, be good, and if someone happens to ask, *then* talk about Jesus?

Evangelistic passivity is not so much a doctrinal issue, it's a coronary one. Our hearts craft masterful arguments for why instead of going to our neighbors, we can simply wait for them to come to us. For many of us, it can feel like a win simply to convince our neighbors that we work hard or that we're not weird.

PERSONAL EVANGELISM IN A POST-CHRISTIAN CULTURE

Nearly 20 years ago in Boston, where I serve, a religious sex scandal of epic proportions shocked the city and the world. To this day, suspicion of religious leaders hangs in the air. Many make no distinction between different kinds of religious leaders—evidenced by how many times in a month I'm referred to as a priest. Eyebrows raise when I tell folks I'm a pastor. Amid a post-Christian culture that harbors suspicion toward pastors, it can be easy to turn the wheel of the ship just a few clicks and spend our days building up a good reputation, but never getting to the gospel.

Many of us who preach the cross from our pulpits from week to week give ourselves a free pass on personal evangelism. This deception is so subtle precisely because we may find ourselves justifying our silence while staring at that glorious mandate in 2 Timothy 4:5: "Do the work of an evangelist."

But lest we forget, the man who wrote those words shared the Evangel not only from pulpits but from prison, while chained to Roman soldiers. Evangelism doesn't get any more personal than that! We may reach fifties, hundreds, or even thousands from the pulpit. But how many pastors who preach the gospel in the sacred desk decline to look their neighbors in the eye over the dinner table and tell them how they must be saved?

A GODLY CHARACTER IS NOT ENOUGH

As I savored what my friend with the golden doodles said, I admired the first part of it—yes, as pastors, we must *be good.* The world needs pastors with character, who lead their congregations into sacrificial service. We need to speak and act for the cause of justice in our cities and our churches like never before. As Jesus himself said, "Let your light shine before others so that they may see your good works and give glory to your Father who is in heaven" (Matt. 5:16). We must earn trust in our communities, and that takes time and diligent good works. It's also pretty good advice to avoid, if at all possible, being weird! And of course, we must never stop preaching the gospel from our pulpits.

But we can't stop there.

As pastors, we must bear the reproaches of Christ up close and personal. Scripture indicates that Moses, who saw the cross from afar, counted it as worth more than the treasures of Egypt (Heb. 11:26). For those who stand beneath the cross—who see his nail-pierced hands and feet—are his reproaches of lesser worth now?

DO THE WORK OF AN EVANGELIST

Just over a year ago, my wife Adriana and I found ourselves at our first neighborhood party. Within minutes, I was outed as "a man of the cloth." At one point, as my neighbors leaned in to listen, I said with deadpan seriousness, "I heard that the people in this neighborhood are wicked and sinful, so I was sent here to convert you all to Jesus." I let it hang there for a few seconds and then cracked a smile. People started breathing again. Some smiled and even chuckled. Part of the reason that little statement exploded like an M80 is because it was absurd. No one can convert anyone to Jesus.

But here's where many of my neighbors and I disagree: *God does convert people to him-self.* And he often does it through churches with pastors who *go out* to their neighbors and tell them about Jesus.

I tremble wondering how much wood, hay, and stubble will be rendered on that final day when the Lord examines us and our ministries. How much chaff will pile up where heaps of sapphires and diamonds could've been? Pray for my heart and for these neighbors of mine. Pray that as I sit on the steps of my front porch, I would be compelled by the Spirit to get up, take a walk, and start talking. Pray the same for your pastors.

Dear pastors, do the work of an evangelist. By the grace of God, those whom you are called to lead will fill up the tracks you've made. It will be hard-going, but Jesus is worthy.

ABOUT THE AUTHOR

Jaime Owens is the senior pastor of Tremont Temple Baptist Church in Boston, Massachusetts. You can find him on Twitter at @jaimeowens_.

Send Missionaries & Inspire Senders

John Folmar

As a pastor on the Arabian Peninsula, I am both a goer and a sender. I **went** to the United Christian Church of Dubai (UCCD) in 2005. I'll never forget the support and love of my sending church (Capitol Hill Baptist Church)—praying and even helping me box up my books for shipment, hand-writing messages on cardboard boxes like "May the word of the Lord speed ahead and be honored." I have benefitted from the long-term, loving commitment of a sending church which equipped and prayed and backed us from afar.

At the same time, I am also now a **sender**, charged to equip new leaders who will entrust the gospel to others (2 Tim 2:2). Through our pastoral internship we have trained and sent people who are now serving churches in Jordan, Morocco, Egypt, Somalia, Kazakhstan, Indonesia, India, Nepal, Japan, the UAE, and beyond.

Like all gospel ministry, we have aimed to follow the apostle Paul, whose mission was to "bring about the obedience of faith for the sake of his name among all the nations" (Rom. 1:5). When he wrote Romans, Paul's plan was eventually to stop in Rome en route to Spain: "I hope to see you in passing as I go to Spain, and to be helped on my journey there by you, once I have enjoyed your company for a while" (Rom. 15:24).

Spain was hardly a tourist destination at this point. No plans for windsurfing at Costa del Sol on the Riviera. Paul's purpose was to preach where Christ had not yet been named.

But to get there, he needed Rome—a staging area, a platform to launch him out to the west. Paul needed prayer, finances, people, and logistics. This was what the church at Rome could provide.

Our churches today are called to do likewise.

Here are three practical ways our congregations can be *staging areas* for gospel advancement into the unreached places of the world.

1. SUPPORT FINANCIALLY.

That's what Paul had in mind for Rome: "to be *helped* on my journey there by you..." (Rom. 15:24). The idea of being helped or sent forth suggested financial support, a commonly used term among the early Christian missionaries to send them on their way well-supplied.

You could say that Romans is the greatest missionary support letter in the history of the world.[9] Paul wrote it to introduce the church to his gospel, and then to solicit their support in his missionary enterprise to the west.

All of us are taking a hit financially during the global pandemic. Dubai is especially hard-hit as the price of oil has dropped precipitously, affecting our entire region.

One pastor whose church has been supportive over the years heard about our financial difficulties and emailed me: "We hear that UCCD might be hav-

---

9 https://www.desiringgod.org/messages/make-your-life-count

ing some financial difficulties given the economy in Dubai. Is that true? We'd like to help if we can, but we just want to make sure the rumor we heard is accurate." It was accurate, and they helped us generously, and as a result we met our obligations for the year and continued with our work.

Just consider the selflessness that motivated that email: "We'd like to help if we can."

Now, in the midst of a pandemic, is no time to shave foreign missions support. Of course, for some of us there may be no alternative. However, Jamie Dunlop has argued for prioritizing long-term missions relationships in these days of shrinking budgets: "You don't want to give up 15 years of trust because of short-term budget tightness."[10]

Crises clarify our commitments. Budgets show our ministry priorities. Keep up your financial support of strategic missions work.

2. SEND YOUR BEST.

In Acts 13, the Holy Spirit directed the church at Antioch to "set apart" Barnabas and Paul for missions outreach. Can you imagine losing two leaders of that caliber? What kind of hole would that leave in your ministry? Yet this church was willing to send out productive, powerful leaders to push the boundaries of the gospel farther than they had ever been pushed before. The church at Antioch paid the price to make it happen.

I can testify how difficult it is to send solid servants. In 2010, UCCD sent more than 100 kingdom-minded members, including staff and an elder, to start a new work on the north side of town (Redeemer Church of Dubai). There was an exodus of friendship, energy, ministry, and finances. They had embarked on an exciting mission for God; we were left holding the bag, with empty seats, a stripped-down music team, and muted singing. It was costly and painful.

But over time, as we slowly grew back, we realized that a multiplication of ministry had occurred. The new church was bearing witness on the other side of town and reaching a different demographic. And *we* grew spiritually as a result—with stronger unity and deepened faith as we saw the Lord provide for us through new leadership. Our congregational singing even grew stronger because we had to compensate for diminished musical accompaniment.

Four years later, we had another painful parting with a beloved fellow-elder. Anand Samuel had grown spiritually among us and was trained in our first class of interns. In time, his ministry budded with fruitful discipling alongside pronounced preaching and teaching gifts. We relied on him a lot. Then we were presented with an opportunity to establish a new church in an emirate to the north with no healthy evangelical presence. So we planted another church, led by this brother. Our ministry was stretched, and yet our people were energized by gospel advancement into the next emirate.

In both cases it was a win-win. We had exported many of our most enterprising, faithful members, but somehow we were the ones who were blessed.

Our goal must never be numerical growth, but gospel growth. As Colin Marshall said, "We must be willing to lose people from our own congregation if that is better for the growth of the gospel. . . Some of your best people—in whom you have invested countless hours—will leave you. They will go to the mission field."[11]

This is a sacred responsibility of local churches—whether Antioch then or your church now. We must be prepared to send out our best.

3. HOLD THE ROPE.

When William Carey founded the Baptist Missionary Society and left the English midlands for India in 1793, he was consciously depending on those who sent him.

Carey lacked adequate financial support. He lacked the required immigration permit. He was plunging into an abyss of heathen hostility, with none of the training or support that we have come to rely on in modern

---

10   https://www.9marks.org/article/budgetcovid19/

11   Colin Marshall and Tony Payne, Trellis & the Vine: The Ministry Mindshift that Changes Everything, p. 83.

missions. He would lose wives and children. By all accounts, the obstacles were immense. Six years later, he hadn't seen a single Indian convert. What kept him going?

Back in England, a small band of Baptist pastors had committed to support Carey from afar. Before he left, Carey had enlisted their commitment. As one of them (John Ryland) recalled: "Our undertaking to India really appeared to me, on its commencement, to be somewhat like a few men, who were deliberating about the importance of penetrating into a deep mine, which had never before been explored, [and] we had no one to guide us; and while we were thus deliberating, Carey, as it were, said, '*Well, I will go down, if you will hold the rope.*' But before he went down . . . he, as it seemed to me, took an oath from each of us, at the mouth of the pit, to this effect—that 'while we lived, we should never let go of the rope.'"[12]

It's all too easy to lose interest in supported missionaries who haven't been around for a while. After all, there's so much closer to home, especially in times of financial distress, that demands our attention and prioritization.

How shall we hold the rope for our missionaries?

A. Visit supported workers.

Overseas work can be discouraging. Many times my wife and I have been refreshed by visits from supporting-church elders passing through the region. They cared for us. They asked intentional questions about our marriage, our family, and our spiritual well-being. They prayed for us, and reminded us why we are here. Even now, tears of gratitude well up in my eyes. We were fortified by their encouragement, and we knew the saints back home were praying for them and for us.

B. Extend hospitality to missionaries.

Housing missionaries not only helps them—it helps you. Good things happen when missionaries travel back home. Before seminary, I was deeply influenced by one brother on furlough who had served in Uzbekistan for 10 years. He communicated a compelling vision for missions and planted seeds in my life that would spring up years later. As I learned about the challenges and opportunities of his ministry, I was burdened to pray specifically and regularly for a Muslim family who lived across the street from them. Years later, I learned that they had been converted.

After I joined CHBC's staff in 2003, I first met Mack Stiles as a result of our church's hospitality. I recall it was during the dead of winter. Clouds had prevailed for weeks. Most of us were looking pale and pasty, but Mack somehow was marvelously tanned and healthy. Only later did I realize—in Dubai the sun shines all the time. Mack had spearheaded student ministry outreach in the UAE, and I was gripped as he spoke of the gospel opportunities there. He cast a moving vision for the strategic priority of gospel work on the Arabian Peninsula. It was then that I began to be interested in the UAE. All because of a home church's hospitality. Eventually, Mack chaired the pastor search committee that brought me to Dubai.

Fifteen years later, I'm on the receiving end of such generosity. My family and I have benefitted from countless expressions of loving care—housing, cars, meals, friendship. This summer, we are staying several weeks with an elder of Park Hills Baptist Church in Austin, Texas; yet another congregation that has cared and prayed for us.

We hope for opportunities to encourage them, as well.

C. Keep a missions focus.

Andy Johnson has written capably about assessing, equipping, and supporting solid missions work and building a culture of missions-mindedness. Here are four more ways to build up goers and inspire senders.

- *Preach expositionally*. Devoting your church to a global missions week is great, and cherry-picking passages designed to showcase the missionary mandate is fine, but neither of these will inflame a heart for missions the way

---

12 Quoted in John Piper, *Andrew Fuller: Holy Faith, Worthy Gospel, World Mission*, p. 21.

a long-term commitment to consecutive expositional preaching can. My own interest in missions began to grow as I noticed a global impulse woven through the whole book of Isaiah (just read chs. 11, 19, 42, 49, 54, 56, 66) and regularly sat under preaching that emphasized the glory of God and the cosmic purposes of the gospel.

- *Distribute good resources.* Urge your people to broaden their horizons through solid biography and other reading. I remember my pastors commending such classics as: Tom Wells, *A Vision for Missions*; Courtney Anderson, *To the Golden Shore*; Iain Murray, *The Puritan Hope*; and John Paton, *The Autobiography of a Pioneer Missionary.*

- *Pray for supported workers.* Ever since we were members of Clifton Baptist Church during seminary in Louisville, they have sacrificially prayed and supported us. Every year, they contact us for updated prayer requests. At their annual women's retreat, they devote a portion of time to their supported overseas workers, even sending my wife hand-written notes encouraging us with their prayers.

- *Pray for the nations.* I came to faith in a church where the weekly pastoral prayer was, among other things, a *tour de force* of worldwide gospel concern. My priorities and interests were shaped by the things we prayed for. Also emphasized was the weekly corporate prayer meeting, where the entire congregation prayed to "the Lord of the harvest." It was like Antioch, where the first missionary journey had begun. During corporate prayer and worship, the Lord had designated Barnabas and Paul for the work (Acts 13:2–3). Upon completion of the journey, those two reported back to the church in a similar congregational meeting where "they declared all that God had done with them, and how he had opened a door of faith to the Gentiles" (Acts 14:27).

Notice God's sovereign control in it all. Who did all the work, anyway? The Holy Spirit had set them apart, guided their steps, empowered their preaching, and opened the door of faith to the Gentiles.

Missions is ultimately by God and for God. It's by God because he alone empowers it—sending out his people, empowering their message, and opening hearts to respond to it. Missions is for God because God alone receives the glory. No one else. It is our privilege to be along for the ride.

Whether we send or go, we are weak and dependent on the Lord. As William Carey experienced, "When I left England, my hope of India's conversion was very strong; but amongst so many obstacles, it would die, unless upheld by God."[13]

Which is why churches back home must hold the rope. Not just during a season of heightened missions interest, but for the long haul.

13 Quoted in Iain Murray, *The Puritan Hope*, p. 140.

ABOUT THE AUTHOR

John Folmar is the pastor of United Christian Church of Dubai in the United Arab Emirates.

Pastors on Social Media

Jonathan
Leeman

On a recent Zoom call with half a dozen pastors, one raised the vexing topic of social media. Several of his members had urged him to speak up more in response to racial tragedies that had consumed the nation in previous weeks. "I'm not sure what to say or do," he repined. His own thinking about the incident and its aftermath were still in process. Plus, did he have a responsibility to speak out on social media? Was he complicit in the injustice if he didn't speak out? A lot of people had been pointing to quotes from Martin Luther King, Jr. and Elie Wiesel saying as much.

Another pastor immediately sympathized: "Some of my members want to hear more outrage from me. Others want to make sure I don't sound like an echo of mainstream media." He shrugged his shoulders, "I don't think I satisfy either group."

Knowing how to pastor in the age of social media can be bewildering. We feel its opportunities and its perils. We can encourage dozens or even hundreds of people with a tweet. But... we can also pick fights we don't mean to pick. We can stir up foolish controversies. Apparently, we can even lose our church building by "favoriting" the wrong thing.

Yet the topic cannot be avoided. Twitter, Facebook, and Instagram are today's watering holes, taverns, and town squares. As far back as 2013, 70 percent of Christian millennials read the Bible on their cell phone or the Internet, 56 percent would investigate a church's website before attending, and 59 percent sought spiritual content online.

It's not surprising, therefore, that 85 percent of churches use Facebook; 84 percent of pastors say it's their church's primary online communication tool; and 51 percent of churches say that at least one staff member regularly posts on social media.

Church consultants insist that your church must exploit social media because it helps people find you, builds community, displays your church's vitality, meets people where they live, sells your ministry products, provides a venue for announcements, helps you educate and disciple, and so forth.

And it's not just "low church" evangelicals who use social media. The Church of England asked members to post photos of Easter celebration with the hashtag #EasterJoy. Pope Francis invited his 18 million Twitter followers to join him on "a new journey, on Instagram, to walk... the path of mercy and the tenderness of God."

So how should pastors think about their own use of social media?

THE UNIQUE DYNAMICS OF SOCIAL MEDIA

To answer that, it's worth thinking about the medium itself. You've heard the phrase "the medium is the message." How does medium itself impact and shape what we say or do on social media? First, call to mind older mediums of communication, like the book, the newspaper, or television news. Now, in comparison to those, what's unique about social media, and how does that impact the nature of communication? Here are five unique features worth noting.

1. It puts a printing press into everyone's hands.

Social media places a Gutenberg Press in the palm of everyone's hand—the smart phone. It democratizes the publishing industry. It levels the playing field. Your personal Facebook post appears right next to *The New York Times*'s, the disgruntled church member's tweet right next to the president's. By their appearance in the feed, no tweet or post possesses more intrinsic authority than another. All offer an equal claim to defining reality. A woman might spend years earning a Ph.D. in a field, but one clever word of snark from the man who has read one article on the topic divides the crowd and leaves her looking frivolous.

2. It promotes self-expression.

While newspapers have long made room for an opinion page and editorials, social media exists almost entirely for the purposes of self-expression. I post or tweet in order to tell you what I think, I feel, I believe. It provides a venue in which people share about themselves more broadly—from photos of family vacation to a list of schools one attended. Not only is a printing press in everyone's hands, everyone gets to write their autobiography, only this autobiography is live, moment-to-moment, real-time.

No doubt, a person can do all these things—share their opinions and their family vacation photos—in righteousness.

Yet social media also plays to our conceit. It tempts us to think people want or even need to hear our opinions or see our photos. To the extent I neglect engaging with the world "out there" but remain fixed to my screen, I run the risk of defining reality by what's on the screen. Without a doubt, social media is the perfect medium for a society that believes reality is socially constructed.

My posts and my interaction with the pages of others can become my reality: Here is the house décor I love, my top 5 romance movies, my favorite appetizers and desserts, my pet peeves, my reflections on social justice, my opinions on homosexuality and God, my views on the science of a global pandemic. Here is me. Here is the world I know and experience. If you disagree with one of my opinions, I will be tempted simultaneously to take your disagreement personally—to view it as a personal attack—as well as to view your disagreement as irrational because it defies my reality. And the irrational, of course, cannot be reasoned with. It's dangerous. It needs to be castigated, insulted, shut down.

This is true whether I'm talking about the sublime or the ridiculous. In fact, the whole spectrum between these two begins to fuse together because they now belong to the same categories of my reality. I can talk about God or paint colors in the same way, with the same emotion, in this same venue.

3. It removes pre-publication accountability.

Like every other medium of communication and publishing, social media offers accountability. Say something stupid or wrong, and you will be hounded by the mob. You might even be "cancelled." But what's unique is that social media requires no accountability before the "Post" button is hit. There is no editorial oversight. Every man is his own editor and editorial board.

Not only that, the editorial oversight given to books, articles, and newspaper columns demands a time delay. A writer must wait for an editor to read, which means any flash of emotion or cockeyed certainties of 1 a.m. that compel you to write something will have had time to cool with the rising of a new sun. Yet social media allows me to instantaneously announce to the planet every flurry of rage, lust, and disgust. The medium affords no checks. They must come from the user.

4. It merges publishing with town-hall meetings, but with no accountability for the crowd.

Social media does not merely allow people to act the part of a publisher. It allows the crowd to act the part of a congregational church meeting or town hall meeting or even courthouse. When you speak, the crowd can speak back, offering their cheers or their sneers.

The trouble is, the crowd bears no accountability, and they remain relatively impersonal. In a church meeting or town hall meeting, when one person speaks, anyone responding will be held accountable for his or her response. Everyone's names and faces are present. Plus, everyone will hear the back-and-forth of conversation—claim and counter claim—before decisions are made.

On social media, people read a post, offer a comment, and then move on. They engage in drive-by tweeting, or a drive-by trial. The whole court case—indictment, trial, and conviction—occurs in 280 characters. Case closed. A drive-byer's name might appear above the tweet—"Joe Brown"—but that doesn't mean much. Effectively, the tweet or comment comes without any personal context for "Joe"—no body language, no tone of voice, no history of conversations and personal interactions, just the lazy words "No. Just no" or "Do better."

The anonymous or pseudonymous social media account is the source of even more trouble and rancor. At least "Joe Brown" will probably exercise some internal restraint because his name is present. But the pseudonymous individual—"Woke Bloke," "Methodist Mom"—effectively walks into homes, throws a grenade, and then walks out, the whole time wearing a ski mask so that he or she lacks all accountability. Such users, I believe, are irresponsible, cowardly, and faithless, at least insofar as they style themselves as truth-tellers or prophets.

Too bad for the biblical prophets. They couldn't keep those ski masks on! Jeremiah didn't sit in his pit and John the Baptist didn't lay his head onto the chopping block and whisper to themselves, "Wait, I could have used a pseudonym?" They faced jeers and flogging and imprisonment because they awaited a better city; this world was not worthy of them (Heb. 11:16, 36–38).

5. *It cultivates comparisons, legalism, and tribalism.*

Human beings have always been tempted to wear masks, put their best foot forward publicly, and encourage others to think better of us than we actually are. The structures of social media offer a handy vehicle for these base instincts. The teenager and her Instagram account, the young mom and her Pinterest board, the PhD candidate and his list of associations on Facebook, the ministry leader and his tweets offering solidarity—in all these places, one can be tempted to manufacture an outward image or to cultivate a pristine reputation that accords with the times.

Yet it creates a culture of comparison. Another teen sees that account, another mom those pictures, another would-be intellectual that list, another minister those affirmations—and they all compare themselves to one another. She wonders, "Is that the standard?" He asks, "Should I do the same?" We compare the carefully curated outside of other people's lives with the messy inside realities of our own, as I heard a preacher once say.

These comparisons can then become vehicles for legalism—"maybe I need to do a better job creating more holiday traditions for my children like this mom does"—and that legalism gives way to tribalism, since our tribes typically root in our legalisms. My tribe, after all, consists of the people who keep the same rules I keep, value what I value, prove their virtue in the things I count as virtuous—my way of parenting, my politics and party, my lifestyle.

SUMMARIZING THESE DYNAMICS

All five of these dynamics, I'm arguing, are more or less endemic to the structures of social media. Social media platforms—the way they work—democratize publishing, promote self-expression, remove pre-publication accountability, provide the means of meeting-like feedback, and cultivate comparisons which (sometimes) yield a legalistic tribalism. To be sure, the technology is morally neutral. They can be used for the purposes of righteousness or wickedness, like any technology. A person can tweet or post on Facebook for the genuine good of others, exercising a proper restraint on themselves, accepting feedback humbly and graciously, and rejoicing in the victories and virtues of others. Yet every technology offers particular temptations and can encourage certain potentialities to moral, willful, fallen human beings.

What potentialities? In a nutshell, social media creates a space to speak up for the defenseless and a space for all the temptations of foolish and wicked speech because it removes the two things that every other society in the history of the world has used to shape and control public speech: access and authoritative structures. The tribal chief and his tribe, the Greek assembly and its votes, Horace Greeley and the laws of libel, have all had traditions and rules and guidelines for public speech. Yet by clearing so much of this away and granting everyone with Internet access a potentially global platform, it opens up public speech to the foolish and the wise both.

On the one hand, we can more easily heed King Lemuel's instruction:

> Speak up for those who cannot speak for themselves, for the rights of all who are destitute. Speak up and judge fairly; defend the rights of the poor and needy. (Prov. 31:8–9)

On the other hand, the foolish and the wicked are looking through open doors to a wide-open field.

> A fool takes no pleasure in understanding, but only in expressing his opinion (Prov. 18:2).

> Enemies disguise themselves with their lips, but in their hearts they harbor deceit. Though their speech is charming, do not believe them, for seven abominations fill their hearts. (Prov. 26:24–25)

Both kinds of speech have had free reign on this the landscape. And which kind of speech comes more easily in this world? (Admittedly, recent actions by Twitter or Facebook to patrol certain varieties of speech curtail some of this freedom.)

Yet the fact that every one of us now has the ability to comment publicly on our political leaders' job performance, government policy, environmental science, the finer points of Trinitarian theology, the demands of pastoring, the complexities of race, the inequities of the marketplace, the innocence or guilt of the accused, and so much more doesn't mean we have the wisdom and competence to do so. (Read Tim Challies' recounting of the story of Apelles and the presumptuous shoemaker here.)

It's strange to me, however, that so many presume otherwise. It's as if getting a social media platform suddenly makes us all subject matter experts on everything.

This reminds me of something I heard Mark Dever observe recently: our capacities have not increased one bit since the invention of the telegraph, the telephone, or the internet. And people's desires for us to speak doesn't increase our wisdom.

RECOGNIZE THAT SOCIAL MEDIA OFFERS A RIVAL COMMUNITY TO YOUR CHURCH

If that is the landscape, how should pastors think about speaking on it?

Add these five dynamics together and the big picture is this: social media offers a rival community to the local church. It's not the only community or space that does so. Teams, friend groups, CrossFit gyms, and workplaces do the same. Yet social media is a particularly powerful rival because it's self-selected and curated. It offers the voices of authority who tell us what we want to hear and the friends who like what we like. It caters to our natural predilections. It empowers us, giving us a platform for whatever we want. And because it shows up on our phone, it follows us to work, to the grocery store, and into bed.

Such challenges aren't entirely new. Other celebrity voices have challenged the authority of the pastor. Radio and television have long tempted American Christians to heed the counsel of Robert Schuller and Jimmy Swaggert and James Dobson over their own pastors. That said, Schuller and Swaggert never "liked" your post through the television screen, and none of your favorite columnists at your favorite Christian magazine "followed" you. Social media platforms offer you this kind of reinforcement and favor. It also makes social connections and alliances between people that never would have been made otherwise.

Social media is particularly adept at offering a rival disciple (e.g., here)—one that's far more severe and invasive than anything the ol' local church can do. It shames, ostracizes, and vilifies. It costs people their jobs, friends, status, and more. People rightly fear being pulled into its vortex because the crowd lacks accountability, discernment, and love, and it offers no provisions for forgiveness. Political leaders, corporate heads, and ministry celebrities therefore do whatever they can to keep the swarm of digital locusts from descending on them. They'll even bow when required.

The primary thing I'd encourage pastors to feel about social media, in other words, is caution. The crowd will exploit you for its purposes, to say nothing of crushing you. The crowd will also divide your church, whether that means provoking disgruntlement in just one family or stirring up political divides across the congregation. So be on guard, pastor. You're stepping into a dusty Wild West town, and there is no sheriff and no law.

More dramatically, you are wrestling against principalities and powers, and those powers have keen eyes for your desire for a bigger audience and your church members' affinity for other forms of social reinforcement. They want you to believe that other forms of wisdom are more reliable than God's Word, other audiences more important than your humble congregation, other platforms more powerful for speaking, other kinds of impact you can make more lasting and significant. The second you begin to believe these things you have begun to compromise your calling as a pastor.

REMEMBER TO WHOM YOU ARE ACCOUNTABLE—GOD AND YOUR CHURCH

Most crucially, therefore, remember to whom you are accountable as a pastor: first God, second your church. You are not accountable to the world wide web. It did not make you a pastor. You will not give an account for it in the same way you will give an account for your congregation (Heb. 13:17).

Which means, first, that you don't need to speak there. You *need* to speak with your church. And climbing onto one social media platform or another will raise expectations among members of your church that you should use that platform to address the issues of the day. If you don't want those expectations, get off the platform.

If you do choose to step onto a platform, always keep these two audiences distinct in mind: your church and the rest of the internet. As a pastor, you're called by God to speak to the first, not the second. That means you shouldn't feel pressured into addressing everything and everyone on social media. You do have a responsibility as a Christian to speak up, particularly for those who cannot speak for themselves (again, see Prov. 31:8–9). But silence on social media doesn't mean silence on an issue. The ordinary rules of wisdom, stewardship, calling, and moral proximity still apply. Your God-given job is to teach and equip and address any pertinent issues of the day in your church. You might feel called to speak more broadly. You are free to. But you don't need to.

More importantly, the Bible does not require you to use this venue to speak. So brush off anyone who says you "must." Encourage people to say "can" not "must."

On the flip side, precisely because God is your primary audience, you need not be immobilized by fear of social media mobs. Speak what you believe God would have you speak, and let the hurricane winds of opposition blow. If you're trusting and following God, those winds can cause your roots to grow ever deeper into the fear of God. In that sense, learning to speak on social media is a good opportunity for fear-of-God training.

LOWER YOUR EXPECTATIONS AND RECOGNIZE THE MEDIUM'S LIMITATIONS

The vast majority of pastors should probably lower their expectations of what they can accomplish on social media, recognizing the medium's limitations. You're not going to change the world on it. Lower your expectations about the arguments you can win, the persuading you can do, the doctrines you can teach, the justice you can accomplish. Meanwhile, remember that your biblically faithful week-in, week-out preaching *can change* the world for the members of your church.

Am I encouraging pastors to neglect potential stewardships God has given them? Shouldn't we grab *any* platform God gives us? Certainly, pastors should be prepared to preach the Word "in season and out of season" (2 Tim. 4:2). Certainly, the apostle Paul set the example of preaching the gospel in all kinds of places, as should pastors (e.g. 2 Cor. 6:4–10).

Yet we should always fulfill our duties to speak with wisdom, which is why I spent as much time as I did reflecting on the medium of social media. It's not apparent to me that we are persuading others as much as we think we are. The system just isn't built for that. People change their opinions when they listen to voices they trust and when they feel affirmed as God-imagers, which books and articles implicitly offer readers merely by taking the time to lay out an argument. But this system simply offers quick bursts of "WHAT I THINK," which doesn't inculcate trust. Just the opposite: it's rigged to create sparks and controversy. It doesn't reward maturity and nuance so much as it rewards alarmism and hyperbole. A well-meaning Christian might step into this lawless gunslinger's town, burdened by his conscience to speak what is true and just. Yet by opening his mouth he only manages to enflame the battles already underway and get his family and friends shot.

God may have given a few brothers and sisters effective social media ministries. Praise him. But that's harder and rarer than it might look. Most of us would-be truth tellers should know that true words said at the wrong moment or in the wrong way can destroy more than they create (see Prov. 15:1; 25:15; Eph. 6:4; 1 Peter 3:7, 15).

A church, on the other hand, is wired by God to encourage relationships with real people. It's meant to build trust and peace. This is why the Holy Spirit ordered the local church and its structures precisely as he did. He did not go to the trouble of revealing social media in his Word, but our churches. Which domain, therefore, do you think will prove more impactful over time?

I said a moment ago that social media offers a rival community to your church, and rival voices to your own as a pastor. Yet here's a little hunch I have about Christians: the Holy Spirit wires born-again believers to *want* to trust their pastors more than other voices, at least when Christians and pastors are walking in the Spirit (see 1 Tim. 5:17). For instance, a ten-year-old boy is going to listen to his dad explain how to throw a baseball, if he's a good and affectionate dad, sooner than he's going to listen to his baseball coach. I think God designed it that way.

So it is, I think, with pastors and church members. Pastors are tasked with bringing the Word of God. That gives you, pastor, an advantage in the lives of your members over everyone else they're listening to on Twitter or Facebook. Your voice carries a bit more juice. Yet—whoa!—what an extraordinary responsibility that places on you. You must only speak as a pastor where Scripture speaks. You must not abuse your authority by binding consciences beyond your realm of competence and authority. And you must never presume you're capable of changing a heart by leaning on it just enough, as if you were the Spirit. All this will lead to a greater judgment (James 3:1).

WRITE YOUR OWN RULES AND KEEP THEM

What you *must* do—if I might put it like that—is to write your own rules of engagement for social media and keep them.

For myself, for instance, I work pretty hard to stay inside of certain boundaries whenever I post on Twitter. I've not actually written down my rules before, but they've been pretty clear in my mind. Here they are:

1. Stay within my areas of competence.

I feel competent to talk about ecclesiology, political theology and theory, pastoring, several ethical matters, and maybe a few other things. Notice, I didn't say theology and politics. I was more specific. I have a Ph.D. in theology, but even here I'm careful. I didn't feel prepared to wade into the 2017 debate on the Trinity. I read about politics plenty, but you won't hear me addressing the debates on immigration or elections, at least substantively. I could. I have opinions, you know, both on the Trinity debate and the elections! And people might mistake my silence for indifference. But the world wide web is not my responsibility.

2. Avoid controversial topics.

That's not to say I won't address controversial topics in other forums. I've written articles on race, abortion, homosexuality, and complementarianism, for instance. And I've written books on politics. Yet the limitations of Twitter make this a dangerous location to have such conversations. You don't have room to explain, qualify, establish a tone of voice, and so forth. The domain too often creates misunderstandings and unnecessary fights. See also point 4 here.

3. Avoid moment-by-moment commentary on news events.

The rationale of points 1 and 2 both apply here. I thank God for the journalists whose job it is to do this. That's not my job. Summing up all three of these first rules, I'd say more Christians and pastors would do well to heed Paul's words in 1 Thessalonians 4:11: "Mind your own affairs."

4. Speak positively, not critically.

As in point 2, I'm willing to say critical things, but the 280 character-limit makes this difficult to do well. Tweets possess no context for the reader: no body language or tone of voice or room for qualifications, as I've been saying. Furthermore, the general culture of Twitter and civil discourse in America today, I believe, inclines people to read one's tweets and comments in the worst possible light, especially when you say something critical. Bad-faith readings on social media abound, and the mob will quickly assume your motives are nefarious. If "love hopes all things," there's very little love here.

Therefore, I personally choose to avoid critical comments and snark in my Twitter presence. Critical Jonathan needs to go live someplace else. On the rare occasions I do say something critical, I bend over backwards to strike a courteous and affirming tone, even if snark is more fun and my heart wants to do otherwise. "Thanks so much, friend. Your comments really provoke me to think. May I push back on one thing, though?"

5. Speak to edify, not promote myself.

Before I tweet anything, I ask myself, will this edify someone, even a tiny bit? In other words, I use Twitter as an avenue for discipling other Christians. (Due to my job, I don't assume many non-Christians follow me.) Now, I will promote books or other things I've written, and some heart work is involved here. If my gut tells me I'm promoting myself, I don't. Otherwise, I'll risk "sinning boldly," as Luther said. Even when I share light-hearted comments on Twitter, as with a tweet in which I declared Coke Zero the greatest soft drink ever, my goal was to be friendly and warm up the space, if only by one-hundredth of a millimeter. Also, read "12 Questions to Ask Yourself Before Posting Something Online," by Mark Dever.

6. Review resources before retweeting.

Before I commend someone else's article or book, I read all of it. If I haven't, I'll say something to indicate I haven't. "Looking forward to this book..." Or if I don't agree with something, I try to find some way to indicate as much.

7. Always remember the members of my church might be watching.

I don't believe a lot of my fellow members follow me on Twitter, but a few of them do. Therefore, I do my best to never say anything that will jeopardize my pastoral relationship with them.

8. Resist the temptation to tweet regularly, build a presence, and form a community.

If you want to build a brand or increase your followership, you need to establish a consistent "presence." You do this by posting or tweeting several times every day and by replying in friendly fashion to comments. Offering play-by-play commentary on public events, whether playfully on something like the Super Bowl or seriously on traumatic national events, also helps to build a presence. You make yourself a regular voice for your followers. No, I'm not saying everyone who has a social media presence has done this merely to build their brand. People may have plenty of reasons. Yet that's the only reason—for myself—why I could imagine trying to spend more time posting on Twitter. Plus, publishers and ministries and companies and schools all want you to do this, because it helps them.

And, honestly, it's tempting. Maybe building a bigger platform would help 9Marks and give me the opportunity to push the ideas I care about. Yet a couple things have held me back.

First, I don't trust my heart. I'll let God worry about the breadth of my ministry; I'll focus on its depth. Second, I assume I would only be building a community of people who already agree with me. As I've implied throughout this essay, that's what social media does best: clarify and concretize the disagreements that already exist. It doesn't persuade. Any persuading that does occur happens either through bullying and fear, or through the unconscious enculturation we all experience in different environments. I'm not interested in either. Meanwhile, I'd rather spend my time building community and friendships elsewhere—home, church, neighborhood—because that's where I will best grow and help others to grow, including across lines of difference.

Again, no judgment of those who do otherwise. I've been told again and again 9Marks needs a steadier social media presence, and that's probably correct. Perhaps we'll take steps in this direction. I don't know. But for my personal handle, I've resisted social media's unquenchable appetite for the steady and the regular. God doesn't call me to build an audience on Twitter. He calls me to serve my family, my church, and my job.

I say all this about presence, pastors, because I assume the same is *probably* true of most of you. One friend of mine said, if you're not on social media, you don't exist. Okay. There's some truth in that. But I don't want to take that road. And I really hope most pastors around the world don't either. Therefore, I tweet, quite simply, only when there's something I want to say.

There are a few more rules I place on myself, but that gives you the idea. And no doubt these are all wisdom-based principles, not moral absolutes, that work for me. You might have different stewardships than me, but the main thing you should ask yourself is this: *What specifically am I trying to accomplish in this space, given its risks, limitations, opportunities, and tax on other things I might do with my time?*

If you want to build a bigger following quickly, ignore rules 1 to 4 and 8. Present yourself as the subject matter expert on everything, especially the controversial and immediately relevant stuff. You'll attract followers. Plus, if you adopt a critical voice, you'll quickly draw in the choir who is already singing your song. Yet to state the obvious: beware the possibility you might simply be hardening the different tribes against one another and not actually changing anyone's mind.

THE GOOD
AND THE BAD

Here are two things that I think are simultaneously true:

(i) social media has wonderfully helped bring more of the nation's attention to the abuse of women, discrimination against minorities, and other injustices;

(ii) *and* the generally denunciatory and toxic nature of so much social media conversation has damaged the social fabric and unity of the United States and many of its churches, potentially sowing seeds for even more rancor and injustice in the future.

This is what happens when you remove all the boundaries and rules for access to public speech: you get the good and the bad.

My personal rules try to account for both, but, in all honesty, they are probably more calibrated to avoiding the bad. I believe I'm trying to exercise the wisdom of Proverbs and Paul, but presumably my personality and privileges also play a role. You might do a slightly different risk analysis.

One thing is certain, pastor: God is your first audience, your church is your second. Everything else on the internet is negotiable.

ABOUT THE AUTHOR

Jonathan Leeman is the Editorial Director of 9Marks, and an elder at Cheverly Baptist Church in Cheverly, Maryland. You can find him on Twitter at @JonathanLeeman.